BATTLE FOR SURVIVAL

THE TRUE STORY OF RELIGIOUS
PERSECUTION IN JAPAN

BATTLE FOR SURVIVAL
4,536 DAYS IN CAPTIVITY

TORU GOTO

This is the English translation of Mr. Toru Goto's memoir,
originally written and published in Japanese. With Mr. Goto's express permission,
effort has been made to render some passages in a way that makes them
more understandable to readers unfamiliar with Japanese language
and culture, or with the Unification movement and its teachings.

Note: Although the Unification Church changed its name to the
"Family Federation for World Peace and Unification" in 2015,
it is referred to as "Unification Church" in this book for convenience.
Some names of buildings have also been changed.

First edition published in Japanese by Sougeisha

Cover and Interior creative: Jonathan Gullery Design
For this first US edition the cover depicts one of the buildings where
Toru Goto was imprisoned, along with an Indiana sky.

ISBN Paperback 978-1-955414-14-2
ISBN eBook 978-1-955414-15-9

Printed in the United States of America
10 9 8 7 6 5 4 3 2

Contents

Foreword viii

Introduction xiv

Chapter 1: **My Family And I** 2

The Only Place in This World 2

Meeting with Faith 5

A Strange Room and a Heavy Smoker 8

From Hotel to Cat-Dog Apartment 13

Living as Yuji Suzuki 18

Chapter 2: **Complete Collapse** 32

Beyond the Darkness of the Highway 32

The Pastor Who Appeared with a Smile 41

Declaration of Leaving the Church 48

My Father's Death and Return to Tokyo 55

Chapter 3: **I Will Never Die** 66

The Battle with That Man 66

More Escape Attempts 83

Hunger Strike Beginning at Forty 97

Between Life and Death 110

Love Your Enemies 115

Heading to the Shoto Headquarters 122

My Counterattack Begins 141

The Reason I Cannot Forgive 146

Chapter 4: **The Fight To Get It Back** 154

New Start and Criminal Accusation 154

An Unfair Decision 169

One Against Six 180

Mother's Death 189

The Death Throes of the Cornered... 193

The Incomplete Victory in Court 203

The Battle of Twelve Years and

      Five Months—Plus Seven Years 206

Chapter 5: **The Abductions and Confinements Have Not Ended** 218

A Chronology of the 12 Years and 5 Months
of Abduction and Confinement 224

Acknowledgments 227

Foreword

Having served in the United States Congress for three decades, one of the most important things I learned was that religious freedom is the fundamental foundation of all freedoms. Without religious freedom, the freedoms of speech, conscience, and all other liberties are compromised.

When a nation stands against religious freedom, human rights and human dignity are also lost. Sadly, many nations today deny religious freedom, even though the result is persecution, rejection, imprisonment, and many times, even death of the believers.

History teaches us that when a government claims that it is the supreme power above religion and faith in God, then the government can become totally committed to using any means necessary to oppress or even destroy anyone who opposes. We have seen the horrific results of the mass execution of the Jews under Hitler in Nazi Germany and the persecution of the Uyghurs in China. Today, a new threat has emerged, as some leading democracies are retreating from their robust protections of religion and faith.

Mr. Toru Goto's carefully-written book is a heart-wrenching account of how people driven by an anti-God ideology can move Japan, one of America's greatest allies, to deny religious freedom.

In the late 1980s, Mr. Goto followed his brother in joining a new church called the Holy Spirit Association for the Unification of World Christianity, also known as the Unification Church. The church's "Divine Principle" presentations, based on the Bible, deeply inspired Mr. Goto, and he felt reborn with a new purpose in life. "It felt as though my once-dead soul had been revived," he wrote. The Korea-based church's first missionaries arrived in Japan in the late 1950s, and it has since grown stronger, with over one million people joining over the years.

But Mr. Goto's story took place in the middle of a fierce and ongoing battle for the political future of Japan.

The Unification Church's strong belief in God led them to become concerned about the growth of communism, which denies the existence of God, especially on Japan's campuses. The church founded the International Federation for Victory Over Communism, which held lectures to counter God-denying Marxism on college campuses. Church members also volunteered to support anti-communist politicians and policies, such as a bill to outlaw foreign spying in Japan.

The work of the Unification Church was so effective that Prime Minister Nobusuke Kishi, the grandfather of Prime Minister Shinzo Abe, became positive about the church's anti-communism and connected them with his Liberal Democratic Party and its anti-communist efforts.

However, this prompted backlash from those who supported socialism/communism in Japan. A lawyer named Hiroshi Yamaguchi formed a group now called the National Network of Lawyers

Against Spiritual Sales (NNLASS or the Lawyers' Network).

To undermine the Unification Church, this lawyer's group encouraged some families to work with professional faith-breakers and a handful of Christian pastors to use forced abduction, confinement and deconversion "to rescue" their relatives from their new faith. According to an article by Patricia Duval in *Bitter Winter* (June 10, 2025), she writes, "The [Lawyers'] Network started to combat the Church actively and, to this end, has been supporting the violent 'deprogramming,' coerced de-conversion from alleged 'brainwashing,' of the Church members since its inception, so that the members successfully 'deprogrammed' could attack the Church in court for damages."

"The Lawyers' Network has been using and encouraging these faith-breaking practices for decades by referring parents opposed to their adult children's faith to deprogrammers and then demanding from the members who finally accepted to recant their faith that they file civil suits against the Church. They had to sue to prove their apostasy and be released from confinement and enforced persuasion," Ms. Duval wrote.

"Based on the tort rulings they had accumulated, those lawyers pressured the government to file for dissolution of the Church, a claim that the Tokyo District Court granted on March 25 this year," she concluded in her article, "Japan: Lawyers, Deprogramming, and the Unification Church Dissolution Case. 1. Kidnapping and Believers."

Police and other authorities didn't intervene in these events because they were considered "family matters."

Today, Ms. Duval also states in her article that an estimated 4,300 adult believers have been forcibly abducted, held captive, and processed through a deconversion horror. Out of these victims, only 1,700 made it back to their faith; the other 2,600 lost their freedom of belief.

In 1995, Mr. Goto became one of these abductees: He was kidnapped and held against his will by his family, who were influenced by these faith-breakers, and they confined him against his will for an unthinkable 12 years and five months. His story includes episodes of violence, petty cruelties, endless sessions with hired faith-breakers, and eventually years of severe food deprivation.

Battle for Survival details Mr. Goto's brutal and difficult battles, in and out of court, and how it changed history in Japan.

This book comes at a most critical time in Japan's history, when it is on the brink of violating the religious freedom of believers of the Unification Church, the Jehovah's Witnesses, and other religions. For three decades, critics of the Unification Church have sought to dissolve the church, but Japanese courts and authorities didn't cooperate because the church and its leaders have never committed a crime.

However, the 2022 assassination of former Prime Minister Abe—by a man whose mother is a member of the Unification Church—gave the church's critics a powerful new way to vilify the church. The Japanese government, encouraged by the lawyers' group, is pursuing the liquidation—which is equal to the elimination—of the Unification Church in Japan. Importantly, the government is relying on tainted cases—*the old civil lawsuits coerced from former believers who were kidnapped, confined and deprogrammed*—to pursue the dissolution.

Mr. Goto's story serves as a warning to everyone who values religious freedom. Communist countries already suppress religious freedoms with impunity, and today some democracies in Europe, Africa, as well as in Japan, are going down that path.

We honor and applaud Mr. Goto for his successful fight and for bringing his book forward at this crucial time when religious freedom is in peril in Japan and many other countries.

Hon. Dan Burton

U.S. Congress, R-IN (1983-2013)

Introduction

I am looking at several photos printed on A4 copy paper. They are pictures of a six-tatami-mat room in an apartment, taken from various angles. The tatami mats have turned a dark brown, the ceiling boards have a wood grain pattern, and the indigo curtains are sooty and faded. A crack about ten centimeters long runs through the frosted glass embedded with a wire grid. These were scenes that had begun to fade from my memory, but as I turn each page, one after another, the painful images vividly come back to life. Everything was exactly as it had been back then.

These are documents from a criminal court case. I applied for access through the Tokyo District Public Prosecutors Office and made color copies of the originals—there are two hundred pages in total. In the center of the cover page are the names of six accused individuals, beneath which is written: "Case Name: Abduction and Confinement Resulting in Injury; Attempted Coercion." The victim in this case—the complainant—is me.

You might find this hard to believe, but I was held in confinement from September 11, 1995, to February 10, 2008—a span of twelve years and five months. From age thirty-one to age forty-four —often considered the prime years of one's life. The place of confinement was not a foreign country or a remote mountain but an apartment on the eighth floor in Suginami, Tokyo, just a seven-minute walk from JR Ogikubo Station, in a building facing a busy main street with constant pedestrian and vehicle traffic. The photos printed in the court records were taken by the Ogikubo Police Department when they conducted an on-site investigation after accepting my criminal complaint.

On January 31, 2011, I filed a civil lawsuit in the Tokyo District Court against my captors. I won both the first trial (Tokyo District Court) and the appeal (Tokyo High Court), with the courts recognizing the facts of my twelve-year-and-five-month confinement and the illegality of the defendants' actions. The court ordered a total compensation of 22 million yen in damages. On September 29, 2015, the Supreme Court finalized a ruling of complete victory.

Twelve years and five months—or 4,536 days of continuous confinement—in the middle of a city. Some may find it hard to believe such a case could even happen, but this unprecedented case of abduction and confinement is an undeniable fact recognized by the courts.

So, who exactly abducted and confined me in that apartment room?

It was my family. My own parents and siblings were the ones who carried out the abduction and confinement.

Upon hearing of a "family that confined someone for over twelve years," one might imagine them as cruel or sadistic, perhaps abnormal people. But my family were ordinary people with common sense. Not gangsters or anything of the sort. Many may wonder whether it's even possible for regular citizens to lock up an adult man in a city apartment for years on end.

The Korean film *Oldboy*, based on a Japanese manga, tells the grim story of a man confined for fifteen years who struggles to uncover the reason for his imprisonment. Such a plot might be believable in the world of movies or comics—but could something like twelve years of real-life confinement actually happen in modern-day Japan?

Moreover, how did my family come to know of techniques for abduction and confinement that ordinary people would never encounter? What gave rise to the intense, even irrational determination to carry out an illegal act like this for such a long time?

The key to answering these questions lies in the notion of "third-party incitement." This incident was not solely carried out by my family. Behind them were individuals who specialized in orchestrating abductions and confinement.

Though the twelve-year-and-five-month-long confinement, followed by seven years of legal battles, began under extremely harsh circumstances, I gradually turned the tide from the depths of despair and ultimately achieved a dramatic reversal and victory. I hope that this account can be of some support to those who are facing lonely and difficult battles in silence.

Chapter 1

My Family And I

The Only Place in This World

Let me introduce my family who confined me.

Both of my parents were born in the early Showa era and grew up in Yonezawa City, Yamagata Prefecture. My father's family ran a Soto Zen Buddhist temple at the foot of the mountains. His father was a distinguished man who taught at a university and authored works on Buddhism. Although my father was the eldest son, he did not inherit the temple. Instead, after graduating from a national university in the area, he joined a major paper manufacturing company.

My mother was the eldest daughter of educators. Her father served for many years as a principal of an elementary school, and her mother was a teacher at an elementary school.

My parents married through an arranged meeting and had three children in the 1960s—two boys followed by a girl. I was born in 1963, the second son of the family. It was a time when the Tokaido Shinkansen was undergoing trial runs and hailed as the "dream super express," the anime *Astro Boy* was being broadcast on television, and Japan's economy and society were on the verge of rapid growth.

After my sister was born, my father was transferred to the company's Tokyo headquarters, and our family moved to the suburbs of the city.

My father was sharp, highly capable, and extremely dedicated to his work. He demonstrated his abilities to the fullest, climbing the corporate ladder and eventually becoming an executive at the paper company. Thanks to his success, the Goto family was not exactly wealthy, but we were financially well-off to a decent extent.

My father, who often said "Study hard," could be strict and scold us harshly, but he also had a friendly side. He would make sushi and serve it to the family.

He loved fishing and hiking, and often took my older brother and me to Okutama. We'd leave early in the morning by train and catch river fish, like hayas and oikawas, upstream in the Tama River. In summer, we'd bring diving goggles and spears, hunt sculpins, and carry them home in a cooler to make delicious tempura.

When catching sculpins, we would peer into the riverbed through goggles with our backs exposed to the sun. My father's back would get so sunburned it turned red, and the skin would peel a few days later. I found it amusing to peel his skin off without tearing it. I gladly volunteered to do it.

Gathering mountain vegetables with my father wasn't just memorable for the heavy backpack filled with *warabi* and *zenmai*, but also by the scenes of our dinner table, where miso soup and ohitashi dishes were made with those wild greens—always accompanied by my mother's warm smile. She was a full-time homemaker and had a personality quite opposite to my father's: gentle, modest, a little anxious, and worried about what people would say, but deeply loving her family and beloved by all.

My brother, four years older than me, often teased me and we sometimes fought. But during my gap year before college, I wrote to him for advice about what department to enter. He had studied architecture at a university in Tokyo and was working for a construction company. He replied promptly with a thoughtful, detailed letter. Encouraged by his advice, I applied to several architecture departments and ultimately enrolled in the College of Science and Technology at Nihon University. I respected him deeply for how sincerely he supported me.

My sister, three years younger than me, was gentle and easygoing; yet, she also had a stubborn strong will. When she was in junior high school, I used to help her study math before exams. I still remember how happy she was when she got good grades and thanked me for the help.

In this way, the five members of the Goto family lived happily together. We were an ordinary family—perhaps even unremarkably so. But it was our one and only place in this world. None of us could have imagined the fierce battles I would later have to wage against my own parents and siblings.

Meeting with Faith

In 1986, my parents were transferred to Osaka and began living in company housing. They rented out our own home, and my older brother, younger sister, and I each started living alone in Tokyo.

I was in my senior year of university. While I was back home in Osaka for summer vacation, I received a call from my brother in Tokyo.

"There's a place where you can learn something really useful. Why don't we go together?" he said.

My brother, though basically earnest, could be a bit of a smooth talker and too trusting, so I was worried that he might have gotten involved in something suspicious. When I told my parents about the call, my father said, "You should go check it out," so I returned to Tokyo thinking, "What a troublesome brother."

At the time, my brother was twenty-six years old and working for a construction company. The "useful study" he mentioned had been introduced to him by a man who approached him while he was waiting for a friend at JR Ochanomizu Station that March. That was how he got involved with the Unification Church.

Following my brother, I visited a place called the "Video Center" on the second floor of a building in Okachimachi, where I was shown an introductory video.

Since my intention was purely to investigate and not to study, I gave harsh criticism to one of the staff, saying like, "This is boring" and "It's so one-sided." When I looked at my brother sitting next to me, he seemed different than usual. Normally he acted like a big brother, but he looked solemn, almost on the verge of tears.

"It'll definitely be helpful in the future—let's study it together."

He pleaded with me, almost as if he were about to fall to his knees in desperation.

I felt sorry for him. Then I thought I would study a little for now, and if it turned out to be a weird place, I could quit and take him with me.

However, once I started studying, I found myself drawn in.

At the time, I was struggling with inner turmoil that I couldn't talk about with even my closest friends or family. Every time I encountered the world's injustices—wars, crime, infidelity—I felt depressed. I mocked myself with, "Well, that's just how people are," but I hated how selfish I was. I couldn't find any hope or value in humanity or life and was constantly plagued by pessimism and a sense of emptiness.

And yet, somewhere deep in my heart, I longed for a noble life and unchanging, true love.

It was during that very time that I encountered the teachings of the Unification Church through my brother. These teachings quenched my parched spirit. The existence of God, that God's purpose of creation was to realize love and joy, that God and humanity were in a parent-child relationship, that human history had been a history of divine salvation—these concepts were deeply moving and unlike anything I had ever experienced before. It felt as though my once-dead soul had been revived, and I became a follower of the Unification Church.

Originally sent by my parents to scout things out and intending to bring my brother back, I ended up joining the church myself—to my brother's great joy. He also reached out to our younger sister—who was in junior college at the time—and brought her into the faith. Within just over a year, all three of us siblings had become members of the Unification Church.

Among us, my brother was the most zealous in his faith. He even considered quitting his job to devote himself fully to church activities. He returned to Osaka with an introductory video and shared his decision to dedicate his life to God with our parents. Though they were shocked and couldn't accept it at first, they were eventually worn down by his overwhelming passion and quietly accepted his choice.

As for me, after joining the Unification Church, I joined the student division and began living in a dormitory called a "home." After graduating from university, I commuted to a major general contractor from the home and spent my weekends doing missionary work.

The "home" was like a training dormitory, and each church district had several of them. On members weekdays, I and other would take the bus or train to go to work or universities and return to the home at night. Since no one was being monitored or controlled, we were free to leave if we wanted.

What set the home apart from a regular shared house was that everyone shared the same purpose and rules of communal life. There were team leaders or section leaders who guided not just me but the whole group. Eventually, I was appointed team leader for about thirty members. I offered advice and guidance on both doctrine and daily life, and when we gathered to sing gospel songs,

I often accompanied on the guitar. Holidays were for worship services and evangelism. Before heading out to evangelize, we would sing gospels and hymns accompanied by guitar. We didn't just sing and preach—we also played games like "picture charades" (a mix of drawing and guessing) and had a lot of fun together.

Except for the worship and evangelism, life in the home was likely not much different from that in a cheerful student or company dormitory.

A Strange Room and a Heavy Smoker

In May 1987, five months had passed since my brother had begun working full-time for the church. When the tenants who had been renting our family home moved out, our father came up to Tokyo from Osaka and contacted my brother, saying, "Let's meet at the house."

My brother left the communal home, saying he would return before midnight, but he never came back. Worse, he became completely unreachable. Some of our church members, who sensed something was wrong, went to his family's house, but there were no signs of anyone being there. Members turned pale, suspecting that my brother had been abducted and confined.

Every Unification Church member knew about the existence of "deprogrammers"—people who specialized in persuading followers to leave the church.

The believers who narrowly escaped such confinement and coercion brought back terrifying stories: forced admissions into psychiatric hospitals, injections and medications administered against their will, and being held captive until they renounced their faith, no matter how much they cried or screamed.

For this reason, nearly all members lived in constant fear of being kidnapped and coerced into abandoning their beliefs.

It was alarming that such "deprogrammers," who plotted and executed such criminal acts, could operate openly, but that was the disturbing social context of the time. As I had just graduated from university and only learned about the Unification Church through my brother, I still couldn't fully comprehend what was happening. At that time, my faith was still shallow and my sense of reality vague. But with my brother's disappearance, it all suddenly became real, and I couldn't stop trembling in fear.

Desperate to find him, I searched everywhere I could think of. Even when someone vaguely suggested he might be in the Kansai area, I headed there, but I still couldn't locate him.

In October—five months after his disappearance—my father contacted me, saying that my brother wanted to see me.

I feared it might be a trap to abduct and confine me as well. But I was deeply worried about my brother and wanted to see him—if he was alive.

The meeting was not to be at our family home, but in Shinjuku. Since there was a risk I might be abducted right on the street, I asked two male church members to accompany me as bodyguards. They were to secretly follow me and intervene if anything happened.

We met at our designated meeting spot, Shinjuku Station, and my father said, "Let's go to where your brother is." Assuming we were heading to a café, I began walking with him. Meanwhile, two of my fellow church members followed behind and kept watching. When we arrived at the Keio Plaza Hotel, my father said, "This is the place." The two church members also entered the hotel with us, but when my father and I got into the elevator, we were separated.

The elevator stopped at one of the upper floors. The hallway was silent as I followed my father to a room. Inside, I found my brother. Seeing him alive and well, I almost burst into tears. My face must have been a mess.

"It's been a while. How have you been?" he said with a serious look.

"Actually, I've decided to leave the Unification Church. I want you to hear me out too," he added.

Since I was emotionally overwhelmed, I didn't immediately register my surroundings, but I quickly realized that the room was no ordinary one. It was what's called a "connecting room"—two adjacent twin rooms linked by a door. It was clearly an expensive room.

As my awareness sharpened, I noticed that the main door had been rigged with a special mechanism so it couldn't be opened from the inside.

I'd been tricked.

Calling me to Shinjuku was a ploy to confine me and force me to leave the Unification Church. I never imagined I could be held captive in a room in a famous hotel in central Tokyo.

My mother appeared from the next room.

Still in shock from being confined, I was in a daze. Just then, through the connecting door, a man entered—followed by a group of unfamiliar people.

He was short and stocky, with a large face and small, sharply slanted eyes. He looked like someone who operated in the shadows, the kind of man to find in the underworld. Introducing himself, "I'm Miyamura," I could tell he was a heavy smoker from the harsh stench of nicotine.

Miyamura—the name wasn't unfamiliar. His full name was Takashi Miyamura. He was known for bringing along former believers he had persuaded to leave the church, treating them like his subordinates.

After ranting about the Unification Church and its leader, Reverend Sun Myung Moon, Miyamura casually pulled out a cigarette and lit it.

He then asked one of the former believers he had brought along, "What does Sun Myung Moon mean to you now?"

The man pointed to the cigarette butts in the ashtray and said with a smirk, "Something like this."

Trapped in the room, I was forced to listen to hateful words against the church and its teachings by Miyamura and the ex-members. Little by little, my mental strength was being worn down, and I thought, "If this continues, I might lose my faith."

Confronted by Miyamura and his followers, I was genuinely terrified.

Not long after they left the room, I became overwhelmed with anger at the trickery and captivity. I locked myself in the bath-room and began screaming, "Let me out! Somebody help!"

The door was unlocked from the outside, and I was dragged back out. I physically resisted my father and brother, but I was outnumbered. Just when I thought Miyamura had already left, he suddenly appeared from the next room.

"What's wrong, Toru?" he said with a cold glance before disap-pearing again.

Realizing that escaping by force was impossible, I begged my parents and brother to let me go, saying I would be fired from work if I kept skipping without notice. My father replied, "Don't worry, I already called your company."

And so, my life in confinement began.

The door leading to the hallway was securely locked with a special mechanism that couldn't be opened from the inside. My family would come and go through the door connecting the two rooms. There was always someone—either my parents or brother—in the next room, and I was sure their door to the hall-way was also thoroughly locked. To escape, I would first need to enter the adjacent room and somehow get my family to unlock the door. It was hopeless.

Had this been a family vacation and we were staying in this "connecting room," the view of Tokyo through the large windows and the tasteful interior might have made for a wonderful experi-ence. But this was a prison. The only freedom I had was to move between the bed and the bathroom.

Desperate to escape, I was seized by the urge to throw a chair through the window. My body moved before I could think—"I'm doing it."

Though I raised the chair, I imagined the shattered glass and the chair plummeting toward pedestrians on the street below. I froze.

Day after day, Miyamura would return with ex-believers, slandering Reverend Moon and repeating vile, unconfirmed scandals.

I felt like I was going insane.

To get out of the room, I had no choice but to pretend I had left the church.

A few days later, I told my brother and parents that I had realized the Unification Church's teachings were wrong. They looked visibly relieved. Maybe because I was still a relatively new believer, they thought I hadn't been too deeply indoctrinated.

I was hoping they would now release me from captivity.

From Hotel to Cat-Dog Apartment

About a week after I was first confined, I could finally leave the hotel.

But my hopes were crushed immediately.

The car that left the Keio Plaza Hotel didn't head toward my home but went in the opposite direction. They said I would be taken somewhere for "rehabilitation," to prevent me from escaping after my supposed renunciation of faith.

The ride didn't take long. The place was a narrow, six-story building with a pet shop on the first floor—what they mockingly called the "Cat-dog apartment." Though I had been released from the hotel, I was now locked in a room in this building.

It was located in Ogikubo, Suginami—the same area where the Ogikubo Glory Church (Jesus Christ Church in Japan) was located. Its late Pastor Satoru Moriyama is said to have devised this method of confinement and deconversion. Miyamura also lived nearby and was closely connected to Pastor Moriyama. They, along with many former believers who had been coerced into leaving the Unification Church, used several apartments in this area for the same purpose. Naturally, I was also taken to the church—Ogikubo Glory Church—and forced to listen to Pastor Moriyama's sermons and attend worship services.

After we moved to the "Cat-dog apartment," my brother, who now believed I had left the church, told me the details of his disappearance.

On the day our father summoned him home, they were walking together when suddenly our father shouted, "Now!" and several strangers jumped out and shoved my brother into a waiting car.

In the car, my brother looked for a chance to escape. But our father and the other men kept eyes on him. The tense silence continued until the car stopped at a railroad crossing. In a split second, my brother rolled out of the car.

A scuffle broke out on the street—he was trying to run while our father and the men were grabbing at him. Someone who witnessed this apparently called the police, and officers rushed to the scene and took my brother to Hachioji Police Station.

My brother explained what happened and begged for help, but the officers believed our father's story instead of his. My brother was taken back and confined in an apartment in Kobe, where Miyamura pressured him to leave the church. He eventually lost his faith.

It wasn't just my parents and Miyamura who were now connected—my brother had joined them too.

At the Ogikubo Glory Church, which facilitated the withdrawal of Unification Church followers, gatherings known as *Mizukuki-kai* (water stem society) were frequently held for families wishing for their loved ones to leave the church. Many former believers who had been persuaded to leave by Miyamura and Pastor Moriyama attended these meetings. Furthermore, at a private residence located near Ogikubo Glory Church, Miyamura conducted sessions instructing families on methods of abduction and confinement.

In the Goto family's case, the uncle on the mother's side—who was a Christian—advised my parents that it would be best for the children to leave the Unification Church. Following his advice, the parents decided to visit the Ogikubo Glory Church.

It was because of everything that had happened between my brother and our parents that I, too, ended up being abducted and confined.

During my "rehabilitation," I was even forced to attend a deprogramming session for a male Unification Church member who was being held in a room of another apartment. I had to play the same role as the people Miyamura had brought into my room at the Keio Plaza Hotel. Seeing this man suffer in confinement right in front of me, I wanted so badly to help him. But if my fake deconversion were discovered, I'd be subjected to even harsher treatment. I couldn't do anything for him.

Some might wonder why I didn't just escape when I had a chance to go outside. But it wasn't that easy. Whenever I was taken out, my father, mother, and brother accompanied me, keeping a constant eye on me.

I had heard of one believer who tried to escape and was chased down by their parents shouting "Thief!" People on the street tackled him and handed him over to the police. No matter how much he tried to explain, the officers sided with the parents' account and returned the believer to the place of confinement. This episode was well known among other members as well.

There were no allies. And there was no room for mistakes. If I failed to escape, the confinement would become even more brutal. I was extremely cautious, taking no risks whatsoever. All I could do was endure—until the moment I was absolutely certain I could get away.

My opportunity came in late November, a month after I was moved to the Cat-dog apartment.

One Sunday, I was taken as usual to Ogikubo Glory Church. The sanctuary looked just the same—high ceilings, the cross on the altar, the organ, rows of seats, the echo of the pastor's voice.

After the service, everyone bowed their heads for prayer. Everyone closed their eyes to pray. That day, by chance, my mother was seated beside me, while my father and brother sat in front.

It had to be now.

I whispered to my mother, "I'm going to the bathroom," got up, and walked out of the building—then broke into a full sprint. The thought that someone might notice and come chasing after me made my legs tremble with fear, and I couldn't run as fast as I wanted. Still, I pushed myself with every ounce of strength I had.

Thankfully, I spotted an empty cab and waved it down. But I couldn't risk getting off at Ogikubo Station, which was only a ten-minute walk away—if they caught up with me, I would be captured again.

"To Asagaya," I told the driver, choosing the station one stop away from Ogikubo to avoid being caught.

At Asagaya Station, I jumped on the Chuo Line, heading for the Unification Church home. Everything around me had changed since I was taken—the weather, the city, the people. But I couldn't afford to care and just focused entirely on escape.

Back at the Ogikubo Glory Church, the moment they realized I had fled, chaos broke out in the sanctuary—like a hornet's nest had been struck. People rushed out in all directions, searching for me. My parents and brother must have been crushed and devastated. And yet, that moment—my escape—made their determination stronger.

I escaped in November 1987. That same year, Nomura Securities became Japan's most profitable company for the first time, and Yasuda Fire and Marine Insurance famously purchased Van Gogh's *Sunflowers* for a record 5.3 billion yen. While the country was in a bubble of wealth, believers like me were trapped in captivity. Increasingly, since the late 1980s—and especially between 1990 and 1992—a total of 941 believers were reported missing. In that sense, Japan's bubble economy was also a "kidnapping-and-deprogramming bubble."

Living as Yuji Suzuki

After escaping from Ogikubo Glory Church and returning to the Unification Church home, I couldn't feel at ease.

My brother knew where I had been staying, and I had no idea when I might be ambushed again by my family, by Miyamura. After consulting with a church leader, I decided to transfer to a different church to avoid being tracked. I moved from the Taitō Church to the Edogawa Church, but I couldn't tell even my fellow believers where I was going. I didn't know who might leak information. And still, I didn't feel safe.

If someone from Edogawa Church were kidnapped and forced to leave the faith, they could reveal my whereabouts. To protect myself, I adopted a common name and started living under a false identity: Yuji Suzuki.

I wanted nothing more than to return to work, but if my family found out where I was, the danger would only increase. In the end, I had no choice but to resign from the major construction company.

Even with all that, I still couldn't feel safe.

Though I began working part-time under my new name, every

time I stepped outside, I found myself scanning for danger. Was that their van parked nearby? Was someone hiding just out of sight, waiting to drag me away again?

People at the church and at my job called me "Suzuki-kun," but I often failed to respond, forgetting it was me. I would realize they were calling me several moments later and then had to hurriedly answer. Each small mistake reminded me of the exhausting reality I was living—running, hiding, pretending. I was utterly fatigued, both physically and mentally. And on top of that, my sister—who was still a believer—was likely to become the next target of kidnapping and imprisonment. It was painful for me, unable to move, to do anything but give her advice.

My fears for my sister became reality in March 1989, just over a year after I was kidnapped and held at the Keio Plaza Hotel. My sister was abducted by our parents and brother, and taken to an apartment in Ogikubo. And just like my brother, she was forced to renounce her faith—under the direction of Miyamura.

Crushed by the regret of not being able to protect my sister and suffocating under the pressure of never being able to let my guard down, I wandered into a bookstore one day. As I flipped through the pages of a book, I found the words of The Constitution of Japan—it contained articles on fundamental human rights and freedom of religion or belief:

Article 11: *The people shall not be prevented from enjoying any of the fundamental human rights. These fundamental human rights guaranteed to the people by this Constitution shall be* *conferred upon the people of this and future generations as eternal and inviolate rights.*

Article 20: *Freedom of religion is guaranteed to all.*

I found myself quietly wondering, "Aren't these rights supposed to apply to Unification Church believers too?" Yes, this wasn't North Korea or China—this was Japan, a modern nation shaped by generations of struggle for democracy, freedom, and human rights. Yet, I was living each day in fear of abduction and confinement, with no peace of mind, not even for a moment. It was as if I had time-traveled to the dark days of the Christian ban in Japan.

That November, the Berlin Wall fell. The world was moving forward in historic ways.

And I? I was still wandering in a maze, with no exit in sight.

In 1992, three years had passed since my sister had been abducted, confined, and forced to abandon her faith. By that time, I had begun using my real name again, but the relationship with my family remained broken, with no sign of reconciliation.

One day, at the church, I was handed a photograph of a woman. The woman in the photo, Ms. A, was a member of a church in Tokyo.

In August, Ms. A and I participated together in an international mass wedding ceremony held in Seoul, South Korea. The ceremony that year was known as the "30,000 Couples Blessing," commemorating the fact that 30,000 couples had been matched and blessed. During the breaks in the ceremony, I shared my story with Ms. A, and she, in turn, spoke openly and sincerely about herself.

At the time, the media was abuzz with scandals about the Blessing Ceremonies, fueled by the participation of celebrities and athletes. The narrative they pushed was that strangers were being forced into marriage without consent.

But in reality, it was nothing like that. People of shared faith, like Ms. A and myself, were introduced to each other, took the time to build understanding, and chose to accept each other as lifelong partners. The Blessing Ceremony was a beginning—a solemn vow between two people to build a happy family together, grounded in shared faith and values. This was the sincere wish of both my fiancée and me.

However, not long after the ceremony, Ms. A went missing during a visit to her parents' house. When I rushed to her home in Tokyo, it was completely empty. It was clear—she had certainly been abducted and confined.

As her fiancé—but not her legal husband—I had no authority to report to the police. When I tried to seek help, they dismissed it as "a family matter" and refused to get involved. Unable to sleep, imagining the suffering she might be going through in confinement, I fasted for a week, praying that she would return safely.

When two months passed without a single day of peace, I was told that Ms. A was staying at a Christian church called Yamura Church in Tsuru City, Yamanashi, undergoing a "rehabilitation" process after renouncing her faith. The pastor there, Kyoko

Kawasaki, was well known among insiders as someone actively involved in deprogramming efforts carried out through abduction and confinement.

I went to Tsuru City in hopes of speaking with Ms. A. But my fiancée had already made up her mind—she had lost her faith and decided to leave the Unification Church. What's more, she told me she was breaking off our engagement. There was nothing I could do but respect her decision.

Not only failing to protect my sister but also losing Ms. A in this way was a deeply bitter experience. People who had once shared the faith were being forced out.

One day, a member who had been deprogrammed but later returned to the church told me, "While I was being held, I saw your brother."

Though my brother and I hadn't seen each other in years, I had heard he had taken a job at a company run by Miyamura. He was now actively working alongside him, helping to persuade Unification Church members to abandon their beliefs. But hearing again that he had been at one of the confinement sites filled me with discomfort. In 1991, a group of forty former believers filed a lawsuit in Tokyo District Court against the Unification Church for their damages—a case that came to be known as the "Give Me Back My Youth" lawsuit. My brother was one of them.

From my brother's captivity and my own in 1987, to my sister's in 1989, and finally of my fiancée Ms. A, in 1992—those years passed as if I was in a whirlwind of activity.

By then, six years had passed since I first found my faith. I had left my job out of fear of being abducted again. After spending time doing part-time jobs, I began dedicating myself to missionary and educational work within the church community. And somewhere in the midst of the fear, isolation, and that darkness, I found something that became my greatest weapon: prayer.

Before I encountered the Unification Church, I had never believed in God—nor had I ever prayed. But through my own experiences, I came to realize something profound: When I prayed, I truly felt heard. Prayer was not just a ritual—it was a deep, personal exchange between me and God. Despite all my shortcomings, I felt the presence of a divine parent who loved and guided me as a child.

Terrified of being in captivity again, I clung to God and prayed with all my strength. Day after day, I shut myself in the prayer room at the church and poured my heart out to God. And in return, I received a clear and simple answer: Even if I were to be abducted again, I had to become a person whose faith could never be broken—no matter the circumstance. The problem wasn't the environment. It was me.

In addition to prayer, I began to memorize the teachings of Reverend Sun Myung Moon, especially his words on *persecution*. I engraved those words in my heart so that I could recall them if I were ever held again.

I also studied the opposition—the people behind the kidnappings and forced deprogramming. I read both the writings of anti-Unification activists and materials from within the Unification Church, comparing them carefully to understand: Who are these people? What do they say during the captivity? Why do so many lose their faith under such pressure?

And then, the mechanism behind abduction and forced deconversion became very clear.

First, I was able to piece together the historical background.

The Unification Church, founded in Korea, was officially registered as a religious corporation in Japan on July 15, 1964. Its founder, Reverend Sun Myung Moon—born in what is now North Korea—proclaimed himself as the returning Christ, the Messiah. During that time, the church rapidly expanded in Japan, particularly among young people in their twenties who were earnestly seeking truth.

The 1960s were a time of renewed tension in the Cold War.

In 1968, the International Federation for Victory Over Communism (VOC) was established as a political organization affiliated with the Unification Church. With the slogan "Communism is wrong," it actively promoted anti-communist campaigns, both within Japan and internationally, aiming to defend all nations from communist revolution.

As the Unification Church emerged as a new religious movement, it began facing opposition from two major fronts: the established Christian community, which regarded Unification Church as heretical, and the leftist groups, who despised the VOC movement. Thus, the anti-Unification front was born.

I came to understand that this was not only the beginning of ideological conflict—it was also the backdrop that led to the rise in abductions and forced deconversions.

Because the Unification Church was a relatively new religious movement and not well understood by the public, it became an easy target for rumors, such as "lynchings happen inside the church," "people go missing," and "members turn into criminals." These accusations stirred deep anxiety among the parents of believers.

By the late 1970s, anti-Unification activists began operating in the shadows as so-called *deprogrammers*, and cases of members being forcibly admitted to psychiatric hospitals became increasingly common.

For example, seven years before I was confined at the Keio Plaza Hotel, another young Unification Church member named Hideo Mima was captured and confined. Today, Mr. Mima is a Tokushima City councilman serving his seventh term (as of 2025). But in 1979, he was tricked by his family and hospitalized in a psychiatric ward with barred windows for eighty-seven days. He was restrained, injected, and given medication against his will. The Unification Church filed a habeas corpus petition to secure his release. He and two female believers who had suffered similar abuse later won a civil lawsuit in which the court ordered the perpetrators to pay a total of 2.5 million yen in damages.

Once the deprogrammers realized that habeas corpus petitions made it risky for them to use psychiatric hospitals for deconversions, they began to use apartments and rented units as the new standard for confinement. That's why, when I was abducted, I was brought into an unfamiliar—and escape-proof—apartment.

By the late 1980s, separate from the Cold War, a new political conflict emerged in Japan: the push for an Anti-Espionage Law.

Alarmed by the growing movement to establish an Anti-Espionage Law—which would criminalize foreign spies in Japan—leftist forces intensified their efforts to destroy their old adversaries, the Unification Church and the VOC. The leftists launched a major public campaign centered around so-called "spiritual sales" (reikan shōhō) to discredit and vilify the Unification Church. At the same time, deprogrammers began operating in a more organized manner, coaching the families of believers to abduct and confine their own children. As anti-Unification Church media coverage gripped Japanese society, more and more worried parents turned to deprogrammers for help—leading to a rapid surge in cases of abductions. Many deprogrammers were Christian pastors.

If believers managed to escape their captors, they could take legal action against them. So, to avoid the risk of lawsuits, a new strategy was devised: The believer's own family would be thoroughly educated and trained to carry out the abduction and confinement themselves. Deprogrammers would then come and go under the pretense of acting at the parents' request to pressure the believer into renouncing their faith. Even if sued, the deprogrammers could deny responsibility, claiming, "I was just asked by parents to have a conversation."

Moreover, there were numerous testimonies indicating that large sums of money had been paid to the deprogrammers. These included consultation fees (disguised as seminar dues), execution fees (as gratitude payments), and support funds (such as donations for other deprogramming efforts or for church construction projects).

Then, what exactly happened inside those confinement sites?

Deprogrammers manipulated information to erode believers' trust in the teachings, the church, and its founder. To emotionally break the believer, they would bring in parents, siblings, aunts, and uncles who had cared for them since childhood; beloved teachers; close friends; and even former church members. Those who truly loved and worried for the believer would sometimes, out of raw emotion, cry, shout, and plead.

Into this turmoil, the deprogrammers would quietly whisper: *"How can you speak of love when you are causing your own family so much pain?"*

Many believers had joined the Unification Church out of a sincere desire to honor their families and seek a deeper understanding of love and truth. Yet, under the crushing pressure of captivity, they found themselves unable to distinguish what was true anymore. As a result, around 70% of those who were abducted ultimately left the Unification Church.

It also became clear that Takashi Miyamura was at the center of this deprogramming network. He was not a pastor but rather the president of a small advertising company. Many of his employees were former Unification Church members he had personally deprogrammed—including my own brother. It was said that Miyamura had great confidence in his ability to force Unification Church members to renounce their faith, often boasting to the believers' families, "I will definitely persuade them."

After my brother left the Unification Church under Miyamura's influence, he began spending more time at the Ogikubo Glory Church. He eventually rented an apartment in Ogikubo and started working at Miyamura's advertising agency. There, both through his job and his involvement in deprogramming activities, he effectively became Miyamura's right-hand man.

This led my brother to deeply regret having introduced me and our sister to the Unification Church. Gradually, he made it his personal mission to "rescue" other believers.

The more I learned about the mechanisms behind abduction and confinement, the more weighed down I felt. Yet, at the same time, gathering information and studying the situation sparked a new sense of clarity and determination within me.

I realized that the broken relationship with my family could not stay as it was forever. So, I decided to take the first step toward reconciliation.

One day, during a phone call with my father, the topic of my captivity came up. To my surprise, he promised, "We will never do anything like that again."

While it was still unforgivable that my parents had abducted and confined me, I chose to believe that their actions, however misguided, had been born out of concern for their son's future. From that point on, I made an effort to rebuild our relationship—sending letters, giving birthday gifts, and keeping communication open. Little by little, it began to work. By 1994, seven years after my escape from the Cat-dog apartment, my relationship with my parents had improved enough that I could finally visit my family home again. Now in my thirties, I felt a newfound hope that we could start over as a family, and I dared to believe that my life was still full of possibilities.

In 1995, my brother married a woman six years younger than him. It was a turbulent year, marked by national tragedies like the Great Hanshin Earthquake and the Tokyo subway sarin gas attack. My brother's bride was a former Unification Church member who had been deprogrammed and forced to abandon her faith under the influence of Miyamura and Christian pastors.

Both my brother and his new wife had filed lawsuits known as the "Give Me Back My Youth" cases against the Unification Church in Niigata District Court. In short, two former believers—bound together by their shared anti-Unification activism—had found each other and married.

This connection between my brother and his new wife cast a shadow over my relationship with my new fiancée.

That same year, I participated in the 360,000 Couples International Blessing Ceremony with Ms. B. Because Ms. B had also faced strong opposition from her family, we shared many deep conversations about both our family situations.

When I explained my own family's background—my parents, my brother, my sister, and now my sister-in-law—Ms. B's face gradually clouded with anxiety. Every member of my family was now connected to Miyamura. My brother, sister, and sister-in-law had all been forced to renounce their faith by deprogrammers, and my brother was actively working with Miyamura in anti-Unification Church activities. It would have been strange if she hadn't felt concerned after hearing all that.

But I had something that gave me strength: eight years of experience and knowledge since my first abduction. I had built an unshakable confidence that, no matter what happened, I would never betray God and Reverend Moon.

I told her, "Don't worry. Even if I'm abducted again, I promise I'll come back. Please believe in me."

Hearing this, her face softened a little, and together, we vowed to build a happy future.

The Blessing Ceremony marked a new beginning for both of us. I was thirty-one years old, entering the most vibrant season of my life and filled with dreams and hopes for both work and family.

But even then, unbeknown to me, my family was already preparing for a second abduction—this time planning for something far longer and more brutal. They could never have imagined that it would trigger a battle lasting twelve years and five months.

Chapter 2

Complete Collapse

Beyond the Darkness of the Highway

In August 1995, after participating in the International Blessing Ceremony, I took a new step forward in my life. After the ceremony, there was so much to do—finding a new place to live, registering our marriage, and taking care of countless other things that awaited us.

As I worked through each task with Ms. B, my fiancée, I was living in a church residence in Tokyo called "Hishokan," where I helped educate young believers who had just been introduced to the faith.

One day, in the midst of these busy times, I received a call from my father.

"Come home soon for a meal," he said casually.

"Sure," I replied.

At the time, it had become a habit for me to visit my family every few months, sharing dinner together. Sometimes my father, who loved to cook, would proudly prepare sushi for the family. I always looked forward to those visits.

"How about the 11th?" he suggested.

I glanced at the calendar hanging on the wall. September 11th was a Monday. Since Mondays were "adjustment days," when my schedule was relatively open, I figured I would be free that evening.

"Sounds good," I said.

"Then we'll be waiting for you," he replied.

The home I had spent my elementary and junior high school years in was in a suburb of Tokyo. It was an old house when my parents bought it, and by the time I resumed visiting, they had already rebuilt it.

I had loved the view from the second-floor window of the old house. Below, a vast cabbage field stretched out, beyond which lay a wide lawn and a dense, green forest. In the early mornings and evenings, I could hear the calls of birds, like the Chinese bamboo partridges and the azure-winged magpies, coming from the forest.

There was a pillar next to the bathroom on the first floor, its grain darkened with age, marked with the height of us three siblings— black and red lines drawn over the years. On the wide wooden hallway upstairs, about ten tatami mats in size, my brother, sister, and I would race and play together. Even now, their voices and the sound of our running feet come back to me as vividly as if it were yesterday.

The new house was a charming, two-story home with beige walls and a brown roof, built strongly according to my father's design preferences. As you entered the front door, there was a spacious living room on the right, about eight tatami mats in size, connected by a counter to the kitchen—a living-dining-kitchen space, as they call it. When I was first invited to the new house, I thought to myself: *This design really reflects my father's preferences, as he loves cooking.* It was here, in this cozy living space, that I would share meals and precious family time.

It had been eight years since I was kidnapped and confined at the Keio Plaza Hotel. My father had promised, "We'll never do something like that again." Our relationship had healed enough that I could visit home, share meals, and even laugh together with my family.

And yet, deep down, I could never fully shake the fear: *What if it happened again?* Once a family connected with the deprogrammers, it was common for abductions to be attempted multiple times, even after a failure. Worse still, I had heard no news that my brother had severed ties with Miyamura. It seemed likely that he was still deeply involved in deprogramming activities.

Still, I had had enough of being kidnapped and held captive. I wanted to see the pleasant smiles of my parents and siblings. So, to reassure myself, I chose to believe in them.

They wouldn't do it again, I kept telling myself. And each time I went back home, I let my guard down just a little more.

On the evening of September 11th, I arrived at my parents' home just as the sun was setting. That night, my brother and his wife—newlyweds who had recently moved into a nearby apartment—were also there, gathered around the dinner table. After we finished eating and were sitting together, I was just about to get ready to leave when my father suddenly turned toward me with a serious look on his face.

"Tohru, we need to have a talk," he said.

In an instant, the cheerful mood evaporated. Everyone fell silent, their faces tense. My mother sat with her hands on her lap, frowning and looking down. My brother, his wife, and my younger sister sat stiffly, waiting for my father's next words.

My father continued, his voice trembling with nervousness: "We're all very worried about your involvement with the Unification Church."

Then my brother spoke: "We had hoped you would eventually realize the church's mistakes. We've been holding on with patience, giving you time."

We had discussed the church before, my brother and I—sometimes passionately, sometimes calmly. But tonight felt very different.

My father began criticizing the church in a low voice, and after a silence, he said: "As your family, we just can't stand by and do nothing anymore."

Again, heavy silence engulfed the room.

"Let's go somewhere else," my father said.

"We can talk right here," I replied.

"No," my brother said instead, "We can't talk about this here."

A tense argument ensued.

Suddenly, an older man appeared in the living room—it was my uncle from Yamagata. Seeing his large frame, it was obvious he had been called in to physically prevent me from escaping. I realized instantly: They were going to abduct me by force. Nothing could have prepared me for this. I was overwhelmed by shock and panic gripping me so tightly that I could barely think or move.

It was already past 9:00 p.m. Growing impatient with the deadlock, my sister-in-law suddenly raised her voice, cutting through the heavy atmosphere in the room.

"There's no point dragging this out any longer. Let's just go!"

That was the signal. My brother and father immediately stood up, quickly moving to either side of me and grabbing me under the arms, trying to lift me up. I crouched down and struggled to resist, but then my uncle joined in, and the three of them pulled at me from every direction with overwhelming force. A wave of intense despair pierced through me, and all the will to fight drained out of me.

Completely limp, I was hauled toward the entrance and out the front door. In the light spilling out from the house, I saw a man I had never seen before—around thirty years old—staring at me with a cold, expressionless face.

He was standing just in front of the small garden; beyond him was a low wall and a field. Clearly, he had been stationed there to block any escape through the yard. I realized then that there was no way out.

A van was waiting on the street in front of the house. Once I was shoved inside, the rest of my family climbed in as well. In the driver's seat sat yet another stranger. Later, I learned he was my sister-in-law's older brother. They made me sit in the very back seat, in the center, with my father pinning me from the right and my brother from the left.

My father gripped my arm tightly.

"You're hurting me. Let go of that hand," I said. "You promised you wouldn't do this again!"

But nobody responded.

Feeling extremely angry, I asked him where he was planning to take me. My brother simply muttered, "You'll find out soon enough."

The van merged onto the expressway. But no one told me where we were headed.

How could I escape? If I tried to fight or scream, they would just pin me down and cover my mouth. What else could I do? About two hours into the ride, I started to feel the urge to use the bathroom.

"I want to go to the bathroom," I said.

I expected to be allowed to exit the van and go to the restroom at the parking area. Of course, I really needed to pee, but I figured I could use the opportunity to escape. Even if I was on the highway, I could manage it.

Instead, my brother handed me a portable toilet bag made of vinyl.

"You want me to do it here?" I asked in disbelief.

Looking apologetic, he said, "I'm sorry."

I had no choice. It was the first time in my life I had ever urinated inside a car. Sitting down didn't work, and standing up wasn't an option either. After some awkward maneuvering, I managed to partially stand, bending forward slightly, and relieved myself into the bag. There was a rushing sound and the smell of urine wafted through the air. The humiliation of that moment—being surrounded by my sister-in-law and a stranger—is something I will never forget.

The van continued driving through the darkness of the express-way. Inside, no one spoke. Only the hum of the engine filled the heavy silence. Watching the road signs blur past the window, I realized we were heading toward Niigata.

But knowing that didn't change anything. There was nothing I could do. A crushing sense of despair weighed down on me, and I closed my eyes and prayed silently: "Heavenly Father, I know a harsh battle awaits me. But I will never betray You. I will survive this. Please stay by my side, protect me, and guide me."

After several hours, the van finally exited the highway and rolled onto local roads. It had been four, maybe five hours, since we left my family home in Tokyo. Still gripped tightly by my father, I was pulled out of the van. The town around us—a scattering of houses and office buildings—was silent in the early morning, around 2:00 a.m.

It was clear that standing before me was the place where they planned to confine me.

Flanked by my brother and father, and surrounded by the others, I was shoved into an elevator. Second floor. Third. Fourth. Fifth. Sixth. They marched me down the corridor to the very last door. There was no chance to escape—I was completely boxed in.

They pushed me into Room 607. I heard the door slam shut behind me. A curtain separated the entrance area from the hallway, which led to a sparse room—about twelve tatami mats in size—connected to a small kitchen. In the middle of the barren living space stood a single table, just big enough for two people.

Where was I? Still reeling from the shock of betrayal, I glanced around the room. A large glass door led to a balcony. When I moved closer and looked up at the frame, I noticed something strange—a small, red metal device was mounted there, roughly the size of a business card. No doubt, it was a heavy-duty locking mechanism.

Furious, I snapped at my family, shouting, "You promised you would never do this again!" I pointed at the red locking device attached to the sliding glass door and yelled, "Do you know the meaning of this? Do you think it's acceptable to violate human rights like this? Kidnapping and confinement are crimes!"

My father said quietly, "Yes, I did say that," and added with an apologetic tone, "but we had no other choice."

"This isn't kidnapping and confinement. It's protection," my brother said, his voice disturbingly calm.

Then, as if delivering a final verdict, he continued, "Let me make this clear—we will never forgive this issue. We will not compromise until it's resolved, and you're staying here until then. No matter what it takes, we're going to settle this. You'd better be ready."

I asked, "This is the sixth floor, right?"

"Yeah," he replied. "If you jump, you'll definitely die. You should think about it just enough not to."

My brother's tone was cold and no hesitation.

The apartment was stocked with basic necessities—clothes, food, and other supplies needed for a prolonged stay. However, there was no TV, no radio—I was completely cut off from the outside world.

Before I realized it, it was already 3:00 a.m.

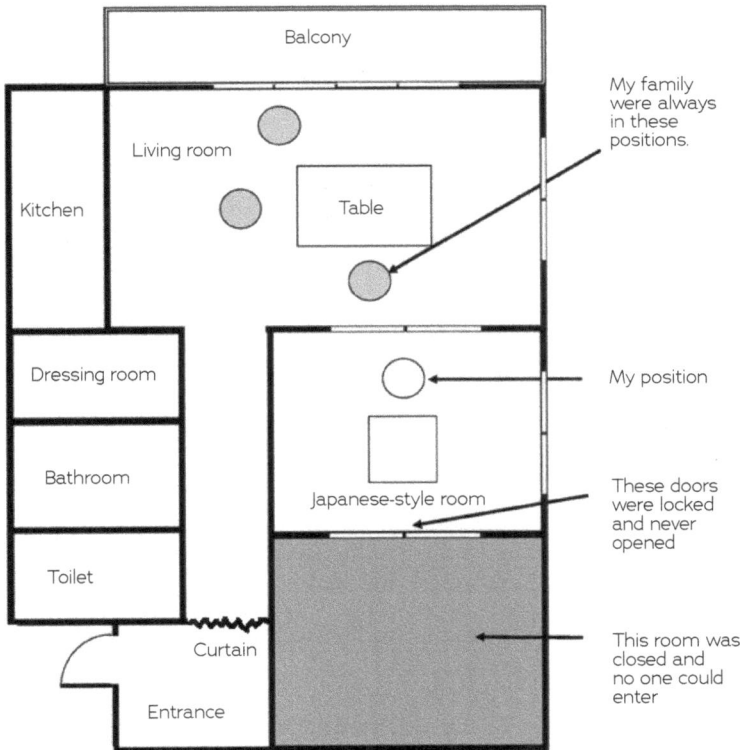

Layout of Room 607, Niigata Palace Mansion

They told me to sleep in the six-tatami-mat room adjacent to the living area. The layout of the apartment was U-shaped, with the hallway, living room, and bedroom connected. When I entered the room, I saw a Japanese futon already laid out.

Looking toward the window, I noticed—just like in the living room—the same red locking device installed on the frame.

They even did it here.

I also noticed a sliding door at the end of the room, leading to what seemed to be another space, but it too had the same heavy-duty lock. I tried pulling on it, but it wouldn't budge.

Why they needed to lock even a sliding door, I couldn't understand. But at that point, I no longer cared. It wasn't just the anger of being thrown into captivity; the traumatic memories of Miyamura's brutal deprogramming from eight years earlier were flooding back. The thought that I was about to relive that nightmare again sent my nerves into overdrive. Even after crawling into the futon, I couldn't fall asleep.

The Pastor Who Appeared with a Smile

"Where am I?"

Still half-asleep, it was as if I had woken from a nightmare—my body was drenched in sweat and I felt awful. But within moments, reality came rushing back. The memories of everything that had happened the day before struck me hard.

I was trapped on the sixth floor of a condominium somewhere near Niigata. It was Tuesday, around 8:00 a.m. By now, the

Hishokan must have been in chaos over my disappearance. My heart ached thinking of how worried everyone must be.

My parents, my sister, my sister-in-law, and my uncle were still in the apartment. Only my brother had returned to Tokyo for work.

I kept asking myself: *Is there any way I can escape?* That was all I could think about.

Even though my brother was gone, there were still five adults in the apartment, including my big, burly uncle. If I tried to scream or struggle, I would surely be overpowered, just like at the Keio Plaza Hotel.

I thought, maybe if I knocked them down, I could escape—but I couldn't bring myself to hurt my own family. Even if I shattered the glass of the balcony door, it's six floors up. If a struggle broke out on the balcony, we could all fall.

No matter how I thought about it, the only chance of escape was through the front door.

The front door stood just beside the bathroom and the toilet. When I went to use the toilet, the watchful eyes on me were so intense that I couldn't even pull aside the curtain covering the front door. But I could tell there was a special locking device installed on it.

As I moved around from the living room to the hallway, the bathroom, I gradually pieced together the layout of the apartment. There seemed to be a door on the hallway side of the "sealed room," directly across from the bathroom. That's why the sliding door leading from the six-mat room to the sealed room had been locked—to prevent any chance of me escaping through it.

When they chose this apartment as the site for my confinement, my family must have carefully planned its use under the guidance of the deprogrammers, checking every vulnerability in the layout. It wasn't hard to imagine my family inspecting the place and discussing—"Let's secure this part" and "We'll block off that area."

No matter how many escape scenarios I ran through in my mind, each one ended with no hope.

After we finished breakfast, my father spoke up.

"Toru, you've always been serious and had a strong sense of justice. If you're willing to dedicate your life to the Unification Church, I want to understand what its teachings are really about. Would you teach me?"

This was a well-known tactic to initiate a forced deprogramming. First, I would be asked to explain the teachings. It would take time, of course, and while I was speaking, the family would quietly listen. When I finished, they would respond with, "We understand your side. Now, please listen to ours." That would be the signal for the deprogrammer to appear.

Refusing to teach, or refusing to listen to their pastors, would not get me released.

On the contrary, it would only prolong my confinement. I had learned that lesson bitterly during my experience at Keio Plaza Hotel and the Cat-dog apartment. In other words, I had no choice.

"Fine," I said reluctantly.

My father brought out a thick book—the *Divine Principle*, the Unification Church's core text.

I asked him to also bring me a notebook.

Soon, we gathered around a low table in the tatami room—my father, mother, sister, and sister-in-law. With the *Divine Principle* and a notebook in front of me, I began to lecture, just as I had when I taught newcomers at the church. I drew diagrams and explained, but the *Divine Principle* is a massive book, nearly 600 pages long, filled with complex terms. Even a broad overview would be nearly impossible to understand without a willingness to learn.

"I didn't quite understand that part," my father would say, and I would explain. We repeated this pattern over and over.

My mother looked distant, her expression blank. She had no interest in the *Divine Principle*; she simply wanted me to leave the Unification Church as soon as possible.

My sister and sister-in-law seemed to listen quietly, but they, too, had already converted to Protestantism after leaving the Unification Church. My explanations must have meant very little to them.

After I had worked through the main points, my father said, with a tone of admiration, "These are actually pretty good teachings."

Of course, I couldn't take his words literally at all. Someone who had gone so far as to confine his own son wouldn't genuinely praise the church's teachings. I knew it was all an act, but trapped as I was, I had no choice but to play along and finish the lecture.

It took me seven days to finish explaining the *Divine Principle*.

During that time, apart from the hours I spent teaching, my family did nothing but watch over me. My days were an endless cycle—get up, wash my face, shave, eat three meals a day, take a bath, and sleep. It might sound like a peaceful routine—but in reality, it was like being forced to dig a hole, fill it, and dig it again, over and over, with no hope of escape.

When I finally closed the *Divine Principle*, my father muttered, "Even after hearing Toru's explanation, I still can't accept it. The teachings themselves might be good, but there are too many problems with the way they actually do things." He was probably referring to the various scandals reported in the media and tabloids. I had my own thoughts on the matter and plenty I wanted to say, but I knew arguing would get me nowhere.

Then my father continued, "Actually, there's a Christian pastor who knows a lot about the Unification Church. I'd like you to hear what he has to say."

Before I could even respond, a man suddenly appeared.

"Hello. My name is Matsunaga," he said, flashing a wide smile.

Unnoticed, he had entered the living room next door and now sat directly across from me at the low table. He looked to be around sixty years old, bald from his forehead to the crown of his head. His smile gave a kind appearance, but when I looked into his eyes, I sensed a bottomless, unsettling darkness.

"You must be Toru-kun," he said. "Your parents asked me to come and speak with you about the Unification Church."

I had heard his name before. Pastor Yasutomo Matsunaga of Niitsu Evangelical Church was well-known, alongside Takashi

Miyamura, for actively participating in faith-breaking activities under confinement.

"Toru-kun, your parents are very worried about you," he said.

"I can't accept what you're doing here at all," I replied.

"I believe the Unification Church is a highly problematic organization. Even the doctrine is nonsense," he shot back.

Pastor Matsunaga pulled a large A5-sized edition of the *Divine Principle* from his bag and placed it on the table. The version most believers carried was usually a smaller, pocket-sized book, but his was larger and so heavily used that every page looked battered and worn.

He flipped through the book, pointing out various passages and criticizing them, and then said, "Please think about this carefully, Toru-kun," before exiting the room. My sister-in-law quickly stood and followed him to the entrance to see him off.

"So, Toru, what did you think of Pastor Matsunaga?" my father asked.

"A pastor who comes to a locked room to convince someone? I can't trust a man like that," I said.

I had my own impressions of Matsunaga, but I kept them to myself. Anything I said would surely be reported back to him. Revealing my thoughts would only give my opponents the advantage.

I understood what Pastor Matsunaga was trying to say: The Unification Church's teachings stray completely from the Bible. The Bible alone is the absolute and complete truth. In contrast, the *Divine Principle* teaches that the Bible is merely one textbook that points toward the truth, not the truth itself. Was that truly correct? These were the points Pastor Matsunaga criticized, leaving them with me as "homework" for our next meeting.

But deep down, I knew there was no real conversation to be had. Matsunaga would only insist that "the Bible alone is the truth" and dismiss any counterargument as "the work of Satan." He would never compromise or reconsider.

That night, lying in bed pretending to sleep, I thought hard about what to do next. Ultimately, the only option seemed to be a "pretended renunciation" again. No matter how much I cried or resisted, as long as I clung to my faith, the captors would never let me go. I knew that too well.

The last time, at Keio Plaza Hotel, escape had been impossible until I pretended to leave the church and was moved to the Cat-dog apartment, where attending a Sunday service at Ogikubo Glory Church had given me my chance. If I could just get outside—even once—there would be a chance to escape.

However, they were professionals in abduction and confinement. A simple act or excuse wouldn't fool them. I had to let them criticize me relentlessly—until they were convinced that I could no longer cling to my faith. They wouldn't be satisfied until they'd pushed me to a point that a normal person would lose their mind. After all, they had once been deceived by my fake renunciation and let me slip through their fingers.

But I've prepared for this. No matter what they throw at me, I won't be broken.

I had already received my answer from God: I must build an

unshakable self who would never betray God or my faith. I had also studied in advance the tactics deprogrammers used to destroy belief during confinement. And most of all, I had to get back to Ms. B, the woman to whom I had pledged my future.

Still, I couldn't deny that after meeting with Pastor Matsunaga, it was becoming harder to control the fear that had taken hold of my heart. The trauma from the brutal deprogramming I had endured under Miyamura at Keio Plaza Hotel was reawakening, stronger than I had realized. It felt like fear was taking one step closer…then another.

The thought that the same torment was about to begin again made me want to scream with everything I had. Even if it wouldn't solve anything, I thought maybe, just for a moment, it could make me forget the fear. But deep down, I knew that if I did, it would only make things even worse with my family.

Declaration of Leaving the Church

As my captivity dragged on, my thoughts kept returning to my Blessing partner, Ms. B. When I had promised her, "Even if I'm abducted again, I will definitely come back," she had looked slightly reassured. I wondered how she was now. I couldn't call her; I couldn't even send her a letter. Even if I could, I didn't even know where I was being held, so there was no way to tell her anything.

Pastor Matsunaga had been visiting about three times a week, each time harshly criticizing the Unification Church and the *Divine Principle*. Without using the intercom, he would knock on the door in a specific, rhythmic pattern—*knock, knock, knock*—like some coded signal. Every time this sound echoed through the room, my family would stiffen and rush to unlock the door, letting him in.

And not just them—I, too, would become extremely nervous, feeling intense discomfort. Even long after my release, just the sound of knocking would trigger the same visceral, overwhelming fear.

As usual, Pastor Matsunaga appeared with a knock, setting down the Bible and the *Divine Principle* on the table, and then he began:

"The word 'Messiah' comes from the Bible. Based on that scripture, explain to me why Sun Myung Moon could possibly be the Messiah."

"If you're going to criticize my faith, then show me something greater than the *Divine Principle*. Otherwise, everyone should be free to believe what they choose," I said.

"I was asked by your parents not to evangelize but to convince you. It's about helping you realize the problems of the Unification Church. That's the whole purpose of this discussion."

"There's no such thing as a 'discussion' in a place where I'm locked up," I replied. "What you're doing is cowardly. At least the Unification Church never locks people up to convert them."

No matter how much I confronted him with the fact and injustice of confinement, Pastor Matsunaga never showed the slightest shame. He would just keep his eyes on the *Divine Principle*.

His criticisms were petty and nitpicky, such as, "How can you not tell the difference between miso and excrement?" or "The *Divine Principle* claims that 'among the doctrines of Christianity, sexual immorality is treated as the gravest sin,' but that's clearly wrong—adultery is only the seventh commandment in the Ten Commandments, not the first."

He also said things like, "The son of a man is a man. The son of a monkey is a monkey. So the son of God—Christ—must be God himself. How could an ordinary human being like Sun Myung Moon possibly be the Messiah?"

Until this point, Matsunaga's arguments stayed within the typical worldview: The Bible alone is the absolute truth. But once he got worked up, he would shout loud enough to shake the entire apartment.

"The Unification Church is a criminal organization! How can someone obsessed with money be the Messiah? He's nothing like Jesus!" he yelled.

It wasn't even an argument anymore—it was just hysterics. And he became impossible to deal with.

Matsunaga often brought former believers with him, or sometimes they came alone. Over time, at least twenty of them visited.

Each one said to me, "I left the church. You should too." Of course, they knew I was being held in captivity. Some might have been attending as part of their "rehabilitation" after leaving the church following their abduction and confinement, or as a test of loyalty, as Pastor Matsunaga asked them to persuade others to leave the church.

One day, when I was in the bathroom, I heard the familiar knock. When I stepped out, tense with nerves, I ran straight into my father on his way to unlock the front door, keys gripped tightly in his hand. In that moment, I realized for certain—the front door, my only possible escape, was also securely locked.

Day after day, in this shut-off world without newspapers or television, I was forced to endure endless criticism. Their method was simple—cut me off from outside information, isolate me, and trample my spirit. I had prepared myself mentally, but the reality was far worse than I had imagined.

I had to pray desperately: "If I can withstand this long enough to fake a renunciation, I will surely find a way to escape. Father in Heaven, please grant me the strength to endure."

Meanwhile, my brother, who worked in Tokyo, would occasionally come to the apartment. Each time, he asked things like:

"What are you thinking right now?"

"What do you think of Pastor Matsunaga's points?"

"Do you still believe in the *Divine Principle*?"

He was trying to gauge whether the deprogramming was working. I knew he was driven by a guilt—guilt for having introduced me and our younger sister to the Unification Church in the first place.

In late December 1995, three and a half months had passed since my captivity. As I washed my face and shaved, I saw the deepening exhaustion reflected in the mirror. By now, it would no longer seem strange if I had lost my faith.

I called my father into the room.

"I've been thinking a lot, and I've realized the *Divine Principle* is wrong," I said, bowing my head and pretending to pour emotion into my voice. "I'm sorry for all the worry I've caused."

"I see. I understand," he replied with a surprisingly flat and casual tone.

Pastor Matsunaga arrived later that same day.

"I heard you've realized it was a mistake, Toru-kun."

"Yes, after much thought, I've concluded that the *Divine Principle* is not the truth."

"What part of it made you feel that way?" he asked, smiling like he had on his first visit, trying to read my expression. I chose my words carefully and explained why I was supposedly leaving the church.

"I see."

"So, what should I do now? Should I write a formal resignation from the church?"

"There's no need to rush. What's more important is that you take time to sort through your thoughts. You must be feeling confused, having realized something you believed in wasn't true."

"Yes, I will."

When I declared that, my father, sister, and sister-in-law didn't show much change in their demeanor. But my mother's face visibly brightened. Seeing her expression made me feel guilty for deceiving my family, even if it was the only way to escape. How devastated she would be if I returned to the Unification Church after a successful escape?

A few days later, my brother visited.

"I heard you've decided to leave the Unification Church," he said, a trace of joy in his voice reflecting his sincere nature.

I wrote a resignation letter and gave it to my father. I thought I'd finally be allowed outside.

But the hope was quickly dashed when Pastor Matsunaga gave me an assignment: "Write a personal testimony about your journey—from joining the church to deciding to leave it." It was clearly a test to determine whether my renunciation was genuine.

I tried to fabricate a story, but no matter how hard I tried, it didn't go well. The experience taught me how difficult and emotionally painful to write something that goes against your heart. So, I turned to the books that were in the confinement room: *Combating Cult Mind Control* by Steven Hassan and *What is Mind Control?* by Kimiaki Nishida. Around this time, the Tokyo subway sarin gas attack by Aum Shinrikyo had made "mind control" a hot topic, and the term was widely used to criticize the Unification Church. It seemed like the perfect theme.

I filled ten pages of report paper of how I had been "mind controlled" by the Unification Church, and how I had come to break free of it, based on the ideas in those books.

Other than the delay in being allowed outside, everything seemed to be going smoothly—until one day, Pastor Matsunaga and some former members visited again.

"Toru, don't you think something's off?" my father said.

Confused, I asked, "What do you mean?" Then he quietly pointed out, "Why are you sitting cross-legged on a chair while Pastor Matsunaga is sitting formally on the floor?"

Startled, I immediately moved the chair aside and sat properly on the floor.

"I'm sorry. I didn't mean to appear arrogant."

Pastor Matsunaga said nothing, simply smiling.

My father had been watching even the smallest details of my behavior. I realized I had to be cautious—not just with my words but with every movement—so that my fake withdrawal would not be discovered.

More than half a year had passed since I claimed to renounce my faith.

Yet, the locks still held firm, and I remained confined in Room 607 of a condominium somewhere in the Niigata area.

The clothes I was given changed from sweatshirts to sweaters as the seasons turned, and by now, it was time to prepare for autumn and winter attire.

Each time my hair grew out, my sister or sister-in-law would cut it. Whether it was because I had no need to go outside or because they used ordinary scissors instead of clippers, the results were always awkward. Not long after I pretended to leave the church, my father brought a television into the room, so I was able to hear and see some information about the world. Even so, I couldn't let my guard down.

How worried must B be right now? She must be desperately searching for me…

The weight of the thought pressed on my chest.

As months of confinement dragged on, the loneliness began to eat away at me, slowly turning into a sense of urgency.

"It's stifling… Please, just let me take a short walk outside," I pleaded with my father. But he refused, "Not yet."

It seemed clear that the failed attempt to monitor me back in November 1987, at the Ogikubo Glory Church, had made my family even more cautious and unyielding.

Spring came again, and the clothes changed back to sweatshirts. In March 1997, a year and a half into my captivity, my father—whose health had been gradually declining—suddenly took a turn for the worse and was hospitalized.

That day, my brother arrived from Tokyo and told me, "Dad has cancer. The doctors say it's terminal. He doesn't have much time left. You should prepare yourself."

"What...?" I gasped.

Without caring who was watching, I broke down and wept uncontrollably.

My Father's Death and Return to Tokyo

A year and nine months had passed since I'd first been confined, and three months had gone by since my father had been hospitalized. One day, as I sat reading the Bible in the room, my sister came in.

"Our brother wants to talk to you."

She was holding something that fit in the palm of her hand—something like a remote control. I intuitively understood that this was one of those modern phones, but I wasn't sure I could use it properly.

"Hello?"

"Toru? Dad passed away today."

My body went limp.

"We're going to say goodbye. Do you want to come here?"

"Where is 'here'?"

"Tokyo."

"…Okay."

Not knowing how to end the call, I simply handed the phone back to my sister.

Obedience to the family was the golden rule for not raising suspicion about fake renunciation. But at the same time, I saw an opportunity—if I was being taken to Tokyo, it might be possible to get outside. I might be able to escape. The very next moment, I was disgusted with myself. How could I even consider using my father's death like that? The shame hit me like a wave.

"Let the dead bury their own dead. You go and proclaim the kingdom of God."

It was a passage from the Gospel of Luke—Jesus's response to the disciple who asked to return home for his father's funeral. I tried to calm myself with deep breaths, but the more I tried, the more tangled my thoughts.

"Shall we go?" my sister said quietly.

My heart pounded. Everything always happened without warning.

I slipped into shoes I hadn't worn in nearly two years and stepped toward the front door. There, three men were waiting: Pastor Matsunaga, a former believer in his twenties who had visited before, and my sister-in-law's older brother.

As I stepped outside, I felt the outside air for the first time in what felt like forever. Guided by the group, I climbed into the rear of a waiting van. Just like during the abduction, they placed me in the middle seat. In the front seats were a driver—a middle-aged former believer—and my sister-in-law. The second row held her two older brothers and another former believer. In the back row, my sister sat to my right, and the young ex-believer to my left. The van, now full, began its journey to Tokyo. Escape was out of the question.

The van kept driving farther and farther away from the apartment where I had been confined. I wouldn't learn until thirteen years later that it was an eleven-story building called "Niigata Palace Mansion," located in Chūō Ward, Niigata City.

A law enforcement official told me this. Had I not filed criminal complaint, I might never have known.

The van arrived at our home in Tokyo.

My brother was waiting outside, and as we entered through the front door, my mother was there. My father's body was laid out in the tatami room next to the one where we had shared a family meal on the first day I was abducted.

On my father's chest, as he lay on a white futon, rested a short ceremonial sword—placed there as a protective talisman to ward off evil spirits. Sitting formally, I gazed closely at his lifeless face. Around us stood the same group who had come with me from Niigata in the van. I paid them no mind; instead, I reflected on my complex feelings toward my father—affection, resentment, respect, all intertwined with memories. My heart was not filled with longing but with bitter regret.

"Shall we go now?" my brother prompted.

As I stood up, I was once again surrounded by family members and former believer, and led back into the van.

"We're not going back to Niigata," my brother said.

I had assumed we were heading back to Room 607, so in a daze, I could only respond, "…I see." What would have happened if I had said no? Most likely, I would've been silenced or scolded.

About thirty minutes later, we arrived at our destination. It was late at night, and the streets were dark. A young woman, illuminated by vibrant neon lights, was standing by the roadside. This unfamiliar woman led me, still surrounded by family, into another apartment.

From Room 607, via my family home, to Room 605—its only known location: somewhere in Tokyo. Like the Niigata apartment, it contained only the essentials—refrigerator, washing machine, and minimal furnishings. Unsurprisingly, there was no television, radio, or, of course, a newspaper.

A curtain hung on the inside of the front door, making it impossible to see the locking mechanism of the door. Just past the entry was a living-dining-kitchen area, along with a bathroom and toilet. Next to the living area was a six-tatami-mat room with a sliding glass door and a balcony. Since we were on the sixth floor, escaping through the windows or balcony was impossible.

"You'll use this room," my brother showed me the six-mat room furthest from the entrance. The living area was always occupied by family members who kept watch over me.

My life in Room 605 was monotonous. Every morning, my brother left for work and returned in the evening. My mother, sister, and sister-in-law stayed in the apartment, handling cooking, laundry, and other housework. With no access to television, radio, newspapers, or even books, I had nothing to do but sit idly every day.

I was concerned about my father's funeral. I kept wondering when it would take place but my brother told me, "You don't need to come."

On the day of the funeral, only my mother and brother went out, leaving my sister, sister-in-law, and me in the apartment. It felt strange that only the eldest son and mother attended the father's funeral while the other children and the eldest son's wife stayed behind. They went to such lengths to keep me under watch, preventing any chance of escape.

A year and a half had passed since my declaration of leaving the church. Despite being confined for a total of a year and nine months, the surveillance remained as intense as ever. When I asked my brother about the whereabouts of my wallet and driver's license, which had been left behind in the Niigata apartment, he dodged the question with a vague, "I don't know." Being completely stuck in an unknown place with nothing, I felt totally helpless and vulnerable.

One day, my family brought me a Bible that had belonged to my father. I decided to take this opportunity to study it and asked my brother for a notebook. I spent my days copying passages from the Bible by hand. Two weeks, then three, passed like that. In the midst of a stagnant situation with no progress or improvement, I felt an increasing urge to take some sort of action.

The only thing I could do was search for clues to escape.

Just like the apartment in Niigata, this one was on the sixth floor, and the glass windows were tightly secured. Seizing a brief moment when I wasn't being watched, I lifted the curtain hanging in front of the entrance door and peeked at its setup. I saw that a dial-type combination lock had been installed the doorknob. There was no way I could get past that.

The prolonged confinement was causing stress to those keeping me captive. Watching me for twenty-four hours restricted their own freedom. They were bound by limitations of both time and space, constantly under pressure. And since what they were doing was against the law, it would be a lie to say they felt no sense of guilt.

One day, as I walked from my room toward the entrance, where the bathroom and toilet were located, my brother suddenly shouted at me, unable to conceal his irritation: "Go back! You're pissing me off!" His outburst filled me with a fear. Simply approaching the entrance seemed to trigger intense stress in him. I think that my brother and his wife, having been forced into this surveillance life with no chance to enjoy their newlywed days, felt like their precious time was being stolen from them.

In mid-December 1997, it had been over six months since I was confined in Room 605.

Late at night, my sister came into the room.

"We're moving to another apartment," she said.

It wasn't a future plan—it meant right now.

The only belongings I had were three notebooks filled with

copied passages from my father's Bible. I gathered them in my hands, and, led by my mother, brother, sister-in-law, and sister, I stepped out the front door. The feeling of putting on shoes after so long felt fresh, but just like when I was taken from the Niigata apartment, three men were already stationed outside the entrance, and the sight filled me with deep exhaustion.

In the elevator, one of the men tasked with preventing my escape struck up a friendly conversation. His face looked familiar—I realized he was one of my brother's high school friends. I assumed they had no choice to recruit someone like him to share in the secret of their criminal act.

It was the middle of winter, and the outside air I hadn't felt for half a year was sharply cold.

The van started moving as my brother urged me inside. I wondered whether we were heading back to Niigata or just relocating somewhere else in Tokyo. But surprisingly, we arrived at our destination very quickly—in less than ten minutes.

As usual, I was surrounded by several people and taken into the entrance of the apartment that stood out with its lights shining in the darkness. We took the elevator to the top floor—the eighth—and walked all the way down the hallway to Room 804.

This new apartment had a rather unusual layout. From the entrance, a narrow hallway stretched about three meters. At the end of it was a six-mat Western-style room. To the right of this room were a 4.5-mat Western-style room; a kitchen; and then a six-mat room, all lined up in succession. Viewed from above, the layout formed an L-shape. The six-mat Western-style room closest to the entrance was separated from the 4.5-mat room by a thick, accordion-style curtain hanging from the ceiling. The kitchen, roughly the same size as the 4.5-mat room, had a gas stove and sink on the left-hand wall, as seen from the Western room, and a bathroom with a toilet and sink on the right. My brother instructed me to stay in the six-mat room at the far end, beyond the kitchen. It felt like the deepest part of a cave.

As my family busily moved around to prepare the room, no one was watching me. I decided to pretend to go to the bathroom and quietly walked toward the front door. My brother was standing in the hallway, and beyond him I saw a door secured with a chain and padlock. When he noticed me, he flicked the back of his hand at me as if to shoo away a stray dog.

"I'm not a dog. I'm a person," I snapped back.

When I returned to the tatami room, my brother came in. "Leave the sliding door open," he said as he reached for the partition between the kitchen and my room. Clearly, he couldn't stop worrying about me.

With the sliding doors fully open, I could see the kitchen. It contained only the bare essentials—a refrigerator, rice cooker, and washing machine. In my room, there were just a low table and a chest of drawers. The far end of this cave was a glass door leading to the balcony, covered with dark blue curtains. As always, there were no televisions or radios.

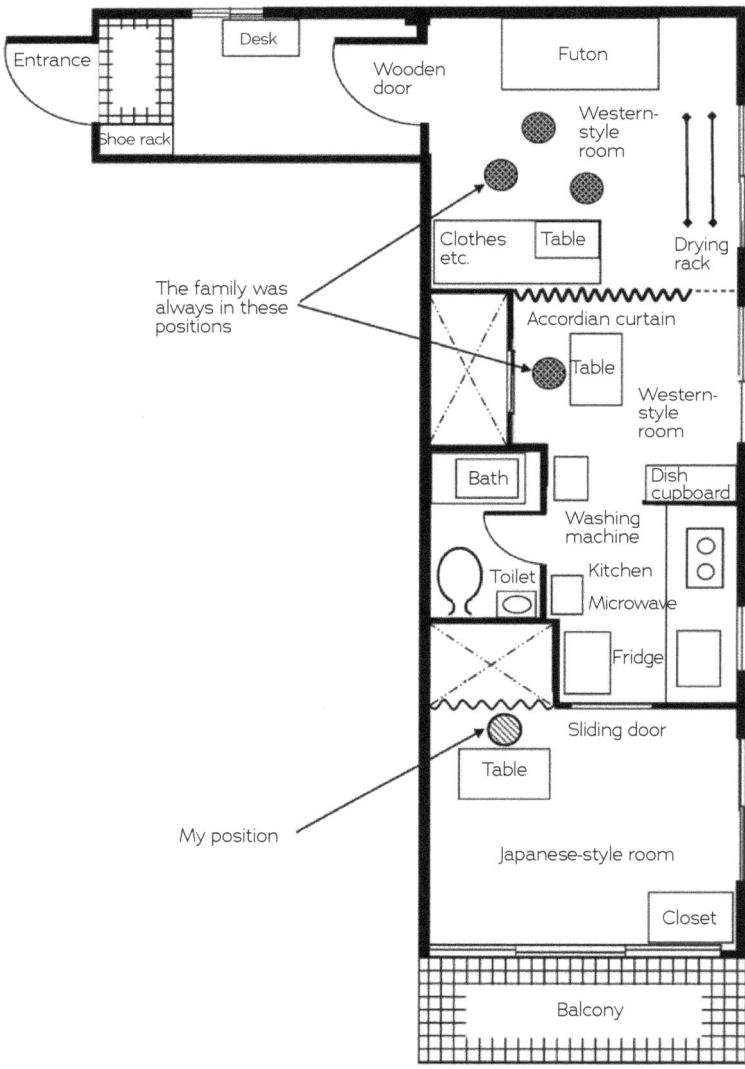

Layout of Room 804, Flower Mansion

No one had explained where we were or why I had been moved. By late at night, my mother and sister began laying out futons in my room. I wondered why they weren't sleeping in a separate room, but I said nothing.

The next morning, they folded the futons and began preparing breakfast in the kitchen. As I had fallen asleep without checking the window, I decided to take a look. I opened the curtains and slid open the shoji screen. The glass of the sliding door was frosted and embedded with wire mesh. Through the hazy, uneven surface, I could just barely make out the vague outline of the balcony.

The balcony spanned the long side of the room, but there was also a smaller window about one meter by two meters on the short side. It, too, had frosted glass, offering no clear view of the outside. What was worse, neither window had the typical latches; both had been replaced with high-security locks that required a key to open the latch.

From the open sliding door, I could see straight into the kitchen, the 4.5-mat room, and the six-mat room, making it clear why Room 804 had been chosen as the new confinement site.

Not only was it nearly impossible to exit through the wire-glass windows with their security locks, but jumping from the eighth floor would mean death. The front door was the only possible escape route. More than that, my life in confinement was confined to just the six-mat tatami room and kitchen for accessing the bath and toilet. If I stepped beyond those areas, it would signal an emergency. Whether my family was in the kitchen, the 4.5-mat room, or the room closest to the entrance, they could immediately detect and block my attempt to escape. Even now, my mother and sister were in the kitchen, while my brother and his wife were in the next room. When I imagined trying to escape, the entrance at the end of the hallway felt impossibly far away.

Looking back, Room 605 must have felt unreliable in many ways. That room seemed to exist solely to absorb the frustration of not just my brother but the rest of the family as well. It was as if I was placed there just to bear everyone's irritation. In contrast, Room 804 was more suited to confinement than even the apartment in Niigata.

Two years and three months had passed since I was abducted from my parents' home. It had been more than two years since I had declared my renunciation. Yet, I had never once been allowed to go outside freely. It felt like my chance to escape was slipping further and further away.

Chapter 3

I Will Never Die

The Battle with That Man

Although the year should be coming to a close, the world within these few meters—formed by the walls, ceiling, and floor—remained unchanged, detached from the hustle and bustle and excitement of December.

My mental state was approaching its breaking point. Pretending to have left the church and hiding my true feelings was taking a heavy toll on my mind. What weighed on me even more was the thought of Ms. B, the person with whom I had made future promises just before being confined. What was she feeling now, and what situation was she in?

When one is faced with loneliness and hardship, there is a weapon available to believers.

Prayer.

A believer turns to God, converses with Him, and receives His guidance.

I had gained insight and courage from God many times before, through deep prayer.

I prayed earnestly. In the bathroom, in the toilet. And, late at night, I covered myself with my blanket and prayed desperately.

Where was God's will? What should I do?

Several days after starting my prayers, I received a clear message: "Declare your faith and battle with honor!"

I was shocked. For two years, I had pretended to leave church to gain freedom, but declaring my faith would make all of that effort useless. Furthermore, if I declared my faith now, it was clear that the intense pressure to renounce it would begin again. Honestly, I thought, "I can't bear this."

But as I continued praying, a verse from the Old Testament came to mind.

"Be strong and courageous; don't be terrified or afraid of them. For it is the Lord your God who goes with you; He will not leave you or forsake you."

This verse, where God encouraged Joshua, Moses' successor, resonated with me deeply. It filled my weary heart with courage, and I made a vow. "I understand, Heavenly Father. I will fight!"

Confident that I had received an answer from God, I immediately took action.

I called my brother into the tatami room, and we sat facing each other across a low table. I looked directly into his suspicious eyes and spoke in a loud voice, so that our mother, sister, and sister-in-law, who were in a nearby room, could hear me.

"The truth is, I was only pretending to leave. I still believe the *Divine Principle* is the truth, and that Sun Myung Moon is the Messiah."

My brother's face darkened rapidly, and his gaze became sharp. I clenched my right hand and slammed it onto the table.

"It's your fault for doing something like this! What do you think you're doing, locking me up like this? Don't mess with me!"

I finally let out the frustration I had been holding in for two years. My brother paused for a moment, then collected himself and spoke.

"I knew it. Your attitude had been a bit indecisive."

The next day, the family's criticism of the Unification Church started again.

After dinner, the family came to my room. My brother began the criticism, and I didn't remain silent. Not only did I rebut their criticism, but I also harshly condemned their confinement actions.

One time, after an intense argument, when I tried to leave the room, my brother grabbed me with both hands. As I tried to escape, he tripped me and knocked me down. I was surprised I could be thrown to the floor so easily, and I couldn't move at all.

"I get it, I won't try to escape anymore, just let me out," I said. He released his grip on me and, giving me a piercing glare, stood up and left

I couldn't stop thinking about how much my strength had deteriorated. For two years and three months, since I had been confined in the Niigata apartment, I had barely walked except when going to the bathroom or the bath. I had spent most of the day sitting down. As a result, my legs and waist had weakened noticeably, and my thighs and calves had become quite thin.

Could I support my 182-cm-tall body with legs that had lost

their strength? This was a serious issue. It wasn't even about breaking through the tightly locked door anymore. Although I had vowed to God I would battle and I eagerly declared my faith, facing the harsh reality of being an infirm man made it feel like all hope had been shattered.

My mental well-being was also eroded by the anxiety of not even knowing where I was. That's why I kept thinking about where I might be.

For instance, was this confinement place in Ogikubo?

After leaving the Unification Church, my brother had found a job at an advertising agency run by Miyamura. He had been involved in persuading members to leave the church. Miyamura's base of operations was his home in Ogikubo, Suginami, Tokyo. The time it took to travel from our family's home to the second apartment, and from there to this apartment, seemed to confirm my suspicions. Furthermore, my family, after failing to convince me to leave the church in Niigata with Pastor Matsunaga's help, probably contacted Miyamura again since he had succeeded in persuading my brother and sister to leave.

Miyamura will probably show up.

This thought filled me with dread, as I remembered his small, narrowed eyes, the smell of cigarette smoke, and his voice and tone. I had been forced to listen to the criticisms of the Unification Church and Rev. Sun Myung Moon, things I didn't want to hear, and those painful memories resurfaced. Even in my dreams,

Miyamura's face haunted me.

It was 1998, and the first three days of the New Year had passed.

"Toru, I need to talk to you," my mother said as she came alone to my room.

"Miyamura-san knows a lot about the Unification Church, right? The family wants you to listen to what he has to say."

Finally, it had come. The tension mounted.

I felt sorry for my mother, who was shrinking and speaking in front of me. I knew she wasn't involved in the confinement out of malice, but because she genuinely cared for her son's happiness. I knew that, in the room beyond the accordion curtain, they must have discussed who would deliver the message, and that my mother must have been chosen.

The verse I had been given in my prayers, "Be strong and courageous," came to mind.

"Alright. I'll listen."

My mother left the room.

"Finally, the battle was about to begin. Please be with me and protect me," I prayed seriously to God.

That evening, Miyamura came into my room with two women who were former believers.

"Oh, Toru-kun, it's been a while," he greeted me.

Has it been ten years? He looked a little older, but his sturdy physique still emphasized his arrogance. Miyamura sat directly across from me at the low table, and in a semicircle, the two women and four family members surrounded me.

"You really just show up like this," I said.

"If I didn't show up suddenly, you guys would run away," he replied, in his usual, mocking tone.

Every time he spoke, the strong smell of cigarettes hit my nose.

"Coward! You ran away that time!"

One middle-aged woman, who sat diagonally behind Miyamura, suddenly raised her voice with a fierce expression. I recalled that she was a former believer who had frequented the Ogikubo Glory Church—she must have been with Miyamura "that time" when I escaped during the Ogikubo Glory Church service ten years ago.

"How many years have they been doing this with the same faces?" she said angrily.

"Calm down," Miyamura said, soothing the woman. He then turned to me. "You want to hear what I have to say, don't you? So, what do you want to hear from me?"

The room fell silent once the woman's shouting stopped.

"My mother asked me to do so. Honestly, I don't want to talk, but I have no choice," I said.

Then Miyamura turned towards my mother.

"Mother, do you think Toru-kun has really left the church?"

"No, he doesn't seem like he's left."

This was typical of Miyamura's method. He changed the atmosphere by asking the family and former believers for their opinions, taking control of the situation.

"You…" he began, his tone now more direct,

"I heard you were pretending to have left the church. Doesn't it hurt your heart to deceive Pastor Matsunaga and your family?"

I didn't answer his question.

"Oh, so now you're silent?" Miyamura pulled out a cigarette, lit it, took a deep drag, and deliberately exhaled smoke, grinning as he did.

"Are you scared of me?" Instead of responding, I stared directly into Miyamura's eyes.

He started by saying, "What will you do if the *Divine Principle* is all a lie? If it's false, you've ruined the lives of the people you educated at the church facility."

When Miyamura finished speaking, another former believer, her face on the verge of tears, spoke out in a voice that sounded as though she was struggling to find the words.

"You've done something terrible. Do you understand that?"

This woman was a senior who had been very kind to me and worked in the same department when I had first converted to the Unification Church. I never expected to meet her again in a place like this.

"Say something! It's no use staying silent!" she cried.

Then the middle-aged woman sitting behind Miyamura got angry and began shouting again.

The room became filled with an eerie atmosphere created by Miyamura and the two women. My mother, brother, sister-in-law, and sister were all caught in the strange air, their expressions stiff.

The loud, middle-aged woman put a cigarette in her mouth and lit it with a lighter. She remained sitting cross-legged, hunched over, with her face down, pursing her lips to exhale a thin stream of smoke like a small pipe. She looked like a woman from a gangster movie. Miyamura, with his own criminal-like demeanor, also kept smoking, and the room was soon filled with a white haze.

After placing his nth cigarette in the ashtray, Miyamura slowly crossed his arms.

"If Sun Myung Moon is the real Messiah and the *Divine Principle* is really the truth, I'll cut my stomach open right here. But if Sun Myung Moon is a fraud and the *Divine Principle* is nonsense, do you have the courage to cut your stomach open?"

He was sounding more and more like a gangster. I had heard before, from the victims of his deprogramming, that this was Miyamura's usual phrase in the confinement room.

After Miyamura made his threat, the two women, who were either angry or on the verge of tears, said what they had to say, and then they all left. The room smelled like ammonia from all the cigarettes.

My brother then came in and said, "Miyamura-san came all this way, so you should at least talk properly. It's rude not to." I had no intention of engaging in a proper conversation since I was being confined. But my brother didn't have any awareness of how they were taking away my freedom and doing something awful to me. It seemed like his sense of reality was completely numb.

From that day on, Miyamura and the former believers started coming around at 6:00 p.m. after dinner, and they would continue their deprogramming efforts for about two hours, until 8:00 p.m. Sometimes there were more people—as many as twelve or thirteen people, such as Miyamura, family members, and former believers—who would gather in my room to confront me. The verbal assaults from all directions felt like a lynching.

They started by attacking the teachings of the Unification Church to make me renounce my faith.

"What's so true about the *Divine Principle*? Explain it to me," Miyamura would say.

When I stayed silent in response to his questioning, he would sneer and say, "Being able to keep believing in something like this is proof that you're mind-controlled."

The discussion on the doctrine went nowhere. Their only goal was to deprogram me, so they had no intention of understanding the doctrine at all.

Their method was to bombard me with one-sided negative information in a closed space, confuse me while numbing my intellect, and at the same time use my family and the former believers to emotionally manipulate me. But since the illegal confinement had been going on for over two years, I wasn't in the mood to listen or debate anymore.

The argument inevitably broke down, and the situation turned into a lynching, with the group overwhelming me by numbers.

I was furious and faced them down, saying, "Let me out of here! You say the Unification Church violates human rights, but the Unification Church doesn't lock people up! It's you who are violating human rights! What do you think freedom of religion means?"

Then Miyamura responded, "Don't talk big. You have no right to claim human rights. And I haven't confined you. Your family is protecting you. If you want to be let out, you should tell your family."

The word "protecting" is a typical term used by deprogrammers to replace "confinement." Miyamura also said, "You're not listening to anyone" and "Use your head, think carefully"—things I must have heard a hundred times.

Each time, I responded by saying, "I am listening" or "I am thinking for myself," but Miyamura stubbornly refused to accept it. In the end, I saw that unless I accepted their criticisms, neither my listening nor my thinking would matter.

I was called "stupid," "fool," and "devil," and finally, I was threatened with, "You can't leave here until you start thinking for yourself" and "If my child ever joined the Unification Church and didn't leave, I'll make a locked room at home and keep them there until they die."

I was privately horrified, wondering what kind of sense of human rights he had.

To make matters worse, Miyamura liked to bring up sex scandals.

"This is a testimony from one of the former Korean top leaders of Unification Church. I'm going to read it to you, so listen carefully."

What he read was something called "blood sharing," which claimed that in the early days of the Unification Church, the founder had sexual relations with followers. None of it could be considered evidence; it was all dubious anecdotes. But Miyamura's storytelling and expressions made it seem believable.

I was furious, blocking my ears to the gossip about my beloved Sun Myung Moon, and I said, "If that's the case, I'll go back to the Unification Church and investigate it myself, so let me out of here."

"You can't do that. The Unification Church always lies. You won't find the truth even if you go back," Miyamura retorted.

Miyamura's talks were full of lies, and as the confinement continued, I was forced to listen to disgusting information I didn't want to hear. Later, after I was freed and returned to the church, I found that the so-called "blood-sharing" story was nothing more than a malicious, baseless rumor. Miyamura's deprogramming tactics were always like this.

Miyamura even used my father's death as a tool for deprogramming. I'm not sure if there was any real connection between my father's death and my refusal to renounce my faith, but it was clear my family suspected that the extreme stress from the deprogramming efforts in Niigata may have played a role in his passing.

"You killed your father," Miyamura told me. "You're the one who killed your father. What are you going to do, now that you killed him?"

Miyamura's heartless words hurt deeply, but I responded angrily, "If you think I killed my father, then take me to the police right now. Let me out!"

Miyamura also often talked about Aum Shinrikyo. In particular, he vividly described how Aum Shinrikyo followers had killed Tsutsumi Sakamoto, a lawyer working on a class-action lawsuit against Aum Shinrikyo, and his wife and child. It seemed as if he was saying, "You're in a dangerous cult too, and you never know when you might do something like this."

Aum Shinrikyo and the Unification Church are completely unrelated, but my mother was terrified by Miyamura's lies, and she kept her head down and sighed repeatedly. It was clear that using the Aum Shinrikyo story as a threat strengthened my family's resolve to never let me escape.

They also controlled information completely. When I asked Miyamura to bring a dictionary so I could look up a word, he flatly refused. On the other hand, he handed me the autobiography of a North Korean defector and said, "You're probably bored, so read this." Maybe he wanted to tell me to wake up like the author did. Only information that supported the deprogramming was allowed to come into the confinement room.

One day, a man appeared who seemed familiar. He was the man who had been standing in the yard when I was kidnapped at my family's home in Tokyo. He also was a former believer and, as it turned out, an employee of Miyamura's company. This confirmed that Miyamura had been deeply involved in my captivity. The former believers who were coming one after another had all been deprogrammed by Miyamura. They interpreted their own experiences of being deprogrammed through abduction as the "right way" and took on the role of "saving poor believers."

Fumiaki Tada, a well-known "critic of unscrupulous businesses" who often appeared on TV, was one of the former believers who visited several times to try and deprogram me.

I could never get used to how my family would suddenly change when Miyamura and the former members came to Room 804. We had been eating dinner together, although it wasn't exactly a peaceful atmosphere. But then suddenly, when Miyamura and his people came in, my family would become emotional and start shouting at me.

One time, when Miyamura, my brother, and a former member all turned against me, I managed to stay calm and unaffected. But then, few minutes later, a dull, metallic screech echoed somewhere in the room. I glanced around, and there was my brother glaring at me like a demon, grinding his teeth.

Suddenly, he stood up and screamed at me, "What's with that attitude! I'd knock you out and nearly kill you!"

I thought for a moment that I might be killed by my brother, who had completely changed.

But before I could even react, my little sister yelled at me, "If this keeps up, you'll be stuck like this forever, so be ready for it!"

I had never seen her like this. Her transformation was even more terrifying than my brother's. It was as if both of them were possessed by different personalities, and it sent a chill down my spine.

The same could be said for one of the former members that Miyamura sent me. She had been gentle and calm when she was a believer of the Unification Church. But one day, she became enraged and told me to "Cut it out!" and threw a cup of hot green tea in my face.

Miyamura and the former believers usually left just after two hours. Meanwhile, my family stayed right in front of me. Once Miyamura and the others left around 8:00 p.m., it became customary for my family to continue the deprogramming session for about another hour, calling it a "review meeting."

During one of these sessions, my brother said relentlessly, "I'm not telling you to quit the Unification Church. But as a family, we can't allow you to be involved in such a problematic organization. So, we want you to become neutral for a while and think for yourself. When you're in the Unification Church, you don't have time to really think. If you still believe the church is the truth, then you have a responsibility to explain it to us. The church has so many problems, so it's natural."

I had no choice but to respond. "You've locked me up, and now you're telling me to become neutral and think? Freedom of belief is guaranteed by the Constitution. This is kidnapping and forced deconversion!"

My brother replied, "This isn't kidnapping and confinement. This is 'emergency protection.'"

I stood up in frustration, ready to leave the room, but before I could take a step, my brother grabbed hold of me, and a fierce struggle ensued. In the midst of the violent tussle, I was forcefully pinned down.

"See? You're using violence to keep me from going outside," I said. "What else could this be but confinement? You're lying if you call this 'protection.' Even if you're family, this is still kidnapping and confinement. It's a crime. If I report this, you all will be criminals. I don't want to make criminals out of you. Please, just let me out of here."

My brother roared back, his voice echoing through the neighbor's house, "Then what other method do you propose? Tell me!" As I stared at him in disbelief, he shouted again, "After everything I've said, you still don't get it? I'm going to make you see reason!" and he slapped my face.

On another day, after the review meeting, I was doing some stretching exercises to relieve the lack of movement and refresh myself when my sister-in-law came into the room.

"How can you do that at a time like this?" she said, speaking in a mocking, annoyed, and dismissive tone.

That was a symbolic moment when I realized I was no longer treated as a person by my family.

One day, I began to feel weak and found it hard to sit still. Thinking I might have caught a cold, I took my temperature. It was nearly 40°C.

My brother said, "It's probably the flu. It's going around. Well, take a little rest."

The source of the infection was unclear, but I suspected that either my family or one of the former believers with Miyamura had brought the virus into my room.

When I fell ill and became unable to move, Miyamura and his followers stopped coming to the room because they were afraid of catching the illness. Fortunately, one of my family members who was going to the hospital gave me some medicine, but that was the only care I received. I realized that unless my condition became severely critical, I wouldn't be taken to the hospital.

Even if I developed a toothache, I knew I wouldn't be allowed to go to the dentist. Just imagining the pain from an untreated toothache was enough to break my spirit. So, I started brushing my teeth carefully, multiple times a day. I had to protect myself at all costs.

Life in captivity was filled with unbearable pain and humiliation, stripped of freedom. On top of that, Miyamura trampled on the sacred beliefs I held. He even used the death of my father as a tool for deprogramming. The suffering I endured was beyond words. At times, I found myself praying for something unimaginable as I lay in bed.

"Dear Heavenly Father, I am sorry. I've reached my limit. I can't bear this anymore. Please, take me to the spiritual world tomorrow without me waking up."

Amid the fear of my mind breaking down and my faith being destroyed, it was prayer and the words of the scripture that protected my heart.

After the first confinement, while fearing the terror of being abducted and confined again, I prayed to God and prepared myself to "never lose my faith." One of the things I did was memorize the words of Rev. Moon regarding persecution.

For example, he said, *"Looking at history, good people have always been struck. Saints have always been struck. If you only look at that, they all seem to have been defeated. However, they were never defeated. They are destined to win the final victory. This is the heavenly strategy. Jesus also took that kind of strategy. Therefore, the path we walk will never be flat. We will walk a path filled with pain and suffering. Those who try to walk a flat path are, without a doubt, rebels against heaven."*

Standing in the midst of adversity and at the peak of loneliness, I recited these words and prayed desperately. Then the wounds of my broken heart started to heal. I was given the strength to stand up once again and confront what lay ahead.

Three months after Miyamura and his followers began coming to persuade me to leave the church, I noticed their expressions changing gradually when I faced them. Not only that, but the frequency of their visits, which had been daily, clearly decreased. I believe my family originally thought, "It's only a matter of time before Toru loses his faith with Miyamura's involvement." However, even though they brought up all sorts of scandals and relentlessly criticized the church, I refused to abandon my faith. Eventually, they ran out of arguments and seemed to tire out.

One day, my brother said, "You are like a black hole. Talking to you drains all my energy."

I believe it was God protecting me.

After September 1998, Miyamura, who had come to Room 804 seventy-three times since the beginning of that year, stopped showing up entirely.

More Escape Attempts

Once Miyamura and the former followers stopped visiting Room 804, it felt as if the energy had drained from the family. It seemed that the failure to make me leave the church using Miyamura, who had been their last hope, had struck them hard.

However, this did not mean they were ready to end my confinement.

The windows remained tightly sealed, and the family's expressions grew even more severe. I didn't think that people who had been hurling manic words at me would simply give up on deprogramming because Miyamura stopped coming. I suspected they were considering other methods to change me.

As autumn turned into winter, 1999 arrived.

Not only did my family speak to me less, but I also ran out of things to say. I spent my days reading the *Divine Principle* and the Bible, as these were the only texts around me. And with no television or radio, I received no information from the outside world. Moreover, without any chance to even go outdoors, I had no way of knowing what was happening even on my street.

The only world I knew was Japan and the world before September 1995. After that, all I had were memories of the three rooms, my family, and the deprogramming attempts. What news did I miss that had shaken the world? The Hanshin-Awaji earthquake, the Tokyo subway sarin gas attack, and the bad loan crisis were among the countless events I never heard about.

A constant question was how was my fiancée, Ms. B, doing?

Years had passed, and so much had changed. People who were

in junior high school in 1995 were now high school students, and those in university studies had graduated and become working adults.

May 1999 arrived. The light pouring into Room 804 became stronger. One day, without notice, my brother brought a small television into my room, plugged it in, and checked that the program was working. Then he left the room.

I wondered if they planned to use it for my deprogramming. I suspected there might be hidden cameras or microphones and approached the TV. It had a fourteen-inch screen with a vertical width of twenty centimeters and was built with a VCR capable of playing and recording tapes. I lifted it up and looked at the bottom, but there were no cameras or microphones.

My brother didn't tell me not to watch TV. But even without suspecting a hidden camera, I couldn't bring myself to turn it on. I felt as though they were trying to condition me to stay in the confined space by keeping me glued to the TV.

At mealtime, my family would come to my room and turn on the TV to watch various programs. They didn't stick to a fixed channel but chose different shows according to the day and time. However, the loud laughter from commercial variety shows and the bright music, sound, and colors from the commercials were not something that could be watched in the heavy silence and tense atmosphere that filled my confinement room.

Eventually, the TV was only tuned to NHK. After meals, someone in the family would immediately turn off the TV and leave the room together. They probably bought the TV to take a break, but watching it together in the confinement room felt so out of place that it had the opposite effect. Outside of mealtimes, no one in the family ever watched TV, and the image of the Japanese-style room was reflected in the dark-colored CRT screen for most of the time.

December 1999 arrived. It had been two years since I was moved to Room 804, and four years and three months since the beginning of my confinement. The period of stagnation had long passed, and it felt like I was being kept alive just to suffer, like an animal trapped in a cage, slowly dying. The frustration I had felt for four years and three months had built up, and with no sign of relief, it was becoming unbearable.

How many times had I dreamed of escaping?

I would look from my room to the kitchen and think, "Can I escape now?" When it seemed impossible to escape, I would consider when I might be able to.

The end of the room near entrance was closed off with an accordion curtain, and I had no idea who might be there.

If my brother was at work, if my sister-in-law was out, and if only my mother and sister were at home, I imagined breaking through their defenses and making it to the hallway. There, I would find a door locked with chains and a padlock. My sister would call my brother on her mobile phone. While I was held up at the front door, my brother, Miyamura, and the former members might gather.

Even though I knew it was futile, thinking of something seemed better than doing nothing. *I can't do anything, but what should I do?*

At this point, I felt that precious time was being wasted with each passing moment, as the day ended and the sun set, making the room dark. It felt like life itself was slipping away.

Every evening, as the day turned to night, I would hear the faint melody of the children's song *Yuyake Koyake* (Sunset) from somewhere. It was being played on the emergency broadcast speakers in Suginami to signal the children to head home, and that one-minute melody gave me some comfort.

To make up for the lost time, I wanted to know what was happening in the world. I didn't want to rely on the one-sided information coming from the TV in front of me. Instead, I wanted to investigate the global situation and Japan on my own, breaking it down like sorting through cities, mountain ranges, and jungles.

I desperately wanted to go to the library, but I knew it was impossible. I thought about asking someone to buy me a book, but just the thought of being rejected made me lose the courage to ask. If my request were denied now, it would feel like losing all hope of living, and I wasn't confident I could keep my mind together in such an extreme state.

On the final days of 1999, as the 2000s were about to begin, I went to the kitchen and called out to my brother in the next room.

"Hey, I need to talk."

It was the first time I had spoken to my family since revealing my fake renunciation.

"What is it?"

My brother, looking puzzled, entered my room, and I asked him to sit down.

"I want a copy of the *Dictionary of Modern Vocabulary*."

I was eager to know about the new events and the words that had come with them. When I finally voiced this desire, my heart pounded with nervousness as if it might explode.

"No."

The refusal came instantly, without any hesitation. The moment his voice reached my ears, something inside me snapped.

"Why not?!"

It had been a long time since I had raised my voice so loudly.

"You don't need it."

A heated argument followed.

"How long are you planning to keep me locked up?"

I couldn't hold back my emotions any longer, and I shouted, "Damn it. I'll leave. I'll jump out of here!" and rushed toward the window.

In my excitement, I had forgotten that the window was locked and wouldn't open. Just as I grabbed the wooden frame of the window, I was yanked backward with immense force. My brother had grabbed the back of my clothes and pulled me in. The wooden frame snapped with a dry sound. I fell backward, and my brother pinned me down, leaving me unable to move.

Two years ago, I had noticed that my thighs and calves had become significantly thinner after being pushed to the ground by my brother, and now, I could feel that my muscles had weakened even further. There was no way to win like this.

"Let go of me," I said.

My brother stood up and left the room.

That night, my anger kept me restless, and I couldn't sleep. My brother seemed unsettled by my behavior and became more cautious.

We entered the new year with this tense atmosphere hanging over us.

A few days later, he showed up in my room and left the latest edition of the *Dictionary of Modern Vocabulary* from the year 2000, which had been released in November the previous year. Shortly afterward, he came back with a copy of the *Sankei* newspaper.

From that day on, someone from the family started bringing the newspaper to my room every day between 10:00 a.m. and 11:00 a.m.

I couldn't believe that my family, who had been so resolute in their refusal, had accepted my request. I almost thought it was a dream. As my confinement continued, my brother, alarmed by my unwavering defiance, reluctantly decided to ease the restrictions.

Whatever the reasons behind it, I had finally gained access to the "present" world.

To make up for the lost years of isolation, I threw myself into reading the dictionary and the newspaper, trying to calm the anxiety that had built up from being out of touch with the world.

Another year passed. By January 2001, the arrival of the 21st century was being reported both on the television and in the newspaper.

During this time, I not only read the dictionary and the newspaper, but I also started copying down the parts that caught my interest in a notebook. However, the more I learned about the current trends in the world and new information, the more my apprehensions grew.

Five years and four months had passed since I was kidnapped at age thirty-one. The 20th century had come to an end, and I was now thirty-seven years old. The crucial years of my thirties, when I should have been gaining social experience and work skills, were nearing their end. That invaluable period of life, which would never come again, was already lost to me. Even though I was in the prime of my working life, time was passing in vain, and I was being left behind by the world, isolated in the confinement room. The world outside, as it moved forward, was pushing me to act.

I couldn't keep going like this. If I didn't take action, I might spend the rest of my life this way. I felt an overwhelming urge to do something.

I decided to take a bold action to regain my freedom.

If I was going to escape, the only way out was through the front door. It was ten meters from my room to the kitchen and then to the entrance. That ten meters felt like a vast distance to me. My family often stayed quietly in the six-mat room closest to the entrance, and I had no idea what they were doing on the other side of the accordion curtains. In any case, I had no choice but to rush through the last room to reach the entrance.

The real issue started here.

It had already been over five years since I disappeared from the Unification Church. Even if I managed to escape, I had no idea where I could go. My wallet had been taken. The only thing I could carry was my underwear.

There was a closet behind where I always sat. Inside it, there was a cardboard box. I thought about putting the underwear in the box to take with me, but it was too large. So, I decided to cut the box and reshape it into a more manageable size.

I asked my brother for some masking tape.

"What do you need it for?" he asked.

"The cardboard box is broken, so I need to fix it."

He gave me a suspicious look, but after a moment, he pulled out about fifty centimeters of tape from the roll, cut it, and stuck it to the pillar next to the closet.

"Is this enough?"

He was cautious and didn't give me the entire roll of tape.

"Just a little more."

He reluctantly tore off another piece of tape and stuck it to the pillar.

"This is all you're getting."

The closet was in a spot that was hard to see from the kitchen side.

Without scissors, I ripped the cardboard box open with my hands, removed the unnecessary parts, and used the tape to assemble a smaller box. I placed my underwear, a shirt, and the notes I had written from the dictionary and the newspaper into the box. After being careful about the weight, I closed the box with the remaining tape and hid it in the closet to avoid being found.

When should I execute my plan? I thought it would be best in the morning, a few hours after my brother left for work.

It was February. The morning of the day I decided to act had arrived.

At 8:00 a.m., we had breakfast as usual. At 10:00 a.m., I took the box I had hidden and held it in both hands. I gathered my resolve, and left my room, stepping into the kitchen. In the room ahead, my mother was sitting. I quickly ran past her, opened the accordion curtain, and entered the six-mat room, where my sister was.

"What's wrong?" she asked surprisingly.

Ignoring her, I hurried through the room and opened the wooden door leading to the hallway.

There, my brother stood.

But I continued to charge forward. Right after, my brother blocked my path, and I was pushed back all the way to the six-mat room. In the next moment, I was thrown to the floor and pinned down. It was the same position as when we had fought before, but I had no intention of giving up just because of this level of violence.

"Let me out! Stop the confinement," I yelled at the top of my lungs.

My brother, holding me down with a furious look on his face, glanced at my sister and said, "Hey." My sister moved to the other side of the accordion curtain.

"Hello? Yes, yes," I heard her voice.

She was probably calling someone.

While I was pinned to the floor, I struggled, but I couldn't move at all. About ten minutes later, Miyamura appeared.

"What are you doing? Stop making noise," Miyamura shouted at me. Seeing that I was restrained by my brother and unable to do anything, he then left Room 804. I remained pinned down for a while, but my brother, seemingly exhausted, eventually released his grip on me.

I returned to my room, still holding the cardboard box.

I didn't know why my brother, who I thought had left for work, was still in the hallway. However, it was clear that he and my sister were able to act quickly and without hesitation because they had likely coordinated with Miyamura for situations like this. It had been a while since Miyamura had shown himself, but it was clear that he still had influence over my family and was giving them instructions.

I had failed in my attempt to escape, but the anger and frustration from the five years and five months of being deprived of my freedom only grew stronger. I could no longer back down.

I'll try to do everything I can.

I made up my mind. I knew it was reckless. However, the burning desire to regain my freedom could not be suppressed.

The only thing I could do was rush toward the front door and scream for help with all my might. If I kept screaming, maybe someone would hear and alert the police. But I had made a vow to myself that no matter what, I would not use violence. I promised myself I would never hit or kick anyone in my family.

At this time, my sister-in-law had health issues and was not in Room 804, so I had to overcome my brother, mother, and sister.

I went to the front door many times a day. Every time my family blocked me, I shouted as loudly as I could, "Let me out!" "Help me!" "Call the police!"

At one point, my brother told me to leave open the sliding door between my room and the kitchen, but I refused, saying, "This is no privacy at all!" and slammed it shut. A little while later, my brother came over and opened it again. I immediately slammed it shut even harder and yelled, "Don't mess with me!" He didn't try to open it again and just went back to the room next to the entrance.

At night, when my mother and sister tried to sleep in my room, I grabbed their blankets from the closet, passed through the kitchen, and threw them into their room.

"I'll sleep alone from now on," I told them coldly. "I'll eat alone. Don't come over here."

To my surprise, my mother, brother, and sister remained calm. They probably anticipated this situation.

I let out all the emotions, telling them, "You claim the Unification Church is violating human rights, but what you're doing is the real violation! The Unification Church doesn't imprison people like this!" "This is torture! It's a modern-day witch hunt!" "How many times have you taken away my right to vote?" "I'll expose the barbaric things you're doing to the world!" "I'll hire a lawyer and sue you. You're the real criminals!"

In normal times, these are words I could never say to my family. However, the people in Room 804—my parents and siblings— were not only my family but also the ones committing the crime of kidnapping. Though it pained me to blame my elderly mother as well, I hardened my heart and threw harsh words at them. Above all, I wanted my freedom and longed to escape.

As I repeatedly tried to escape, my brother stopped going to work and stayed home, watching me constantly.

But I couldn't give up. I kept looking for any chance to rush toward the front door. Every time, my family would restrain me, but I would scream at the top of my lungs, "Let me out!" "Help me!" "Call the police!" In response, they would press a blanket over my face to smother my cries. The fear of suffocating would overwhelm me, and, with what little breath I had left, I would gasp and tell them, "I can't breathe! I'm going to die!" That's when they finally loosened their hold, and I could breathe again.

Having been confined for over five years with little opportunity for physical exercise, my muscle strength had greatly diminished. Whenever I struggled with my brother, he easily overpowered me. Even when my sister and mother held me down, I couldn't move. It was as if they were powered by some force, using incredible strength. I couldn't stand a chance against the three of them.

Our battles were fierce and brutal.

My shirt was torn to shreds, and my body was covered in dark bruises. My face and hands were especially bloodied, as my family scratched and dug their nails into me.

Whenever I rushed towards the front door from my room, I was often stopped in the room before the front door. When I bled during the battle, I would return to my room, wipe the blood off with a towel, catch my breath, and then rush toward the door again. It was a constant cycle.

Some nights, the pain from the constant battles was so intense that it kept me from sleeping, and I would wake up the next morning still in pain. My bruises had spread all over my body, and when I undressed to bathe, I showed my brother.

"Look at this. It's awful," I said.

"Yeah, same," my brother quietly replied.

It made sense that my brother, the strongest person in the family, would bear the most damage. But if that was the case, why didn't he just end the confinement? It felt as if my brother, along with my mother and sister, were driven by a crazed obsession to never let me go. This relentless drive kept them from being able to back down.

One day, while struggling with them, a sharp pain shot through my right hand. I looked down and saw that my ring finger was bent at an unnatural direction. The pain lasted for two or three months, and since my injury went untreated during the confinement, my ring finger has remained permanently bent.

It wasn't just my finger that was broken.

When I grabbed the accordion curtain dividing the two rooms, it tore as my family tried to pull me away. And during the struggle in the kitchen, the metal shelf above the sink bent out of shape.

Our battles didn't end there.

One day, while I was taking a bath, I heard soft voices from somewhere. Straining my ears, I realized it was the conversation of the residents below, coming through the pipes and reaching the "vent" at the top of the wall.

I thought that if I yelled into the vent, my voice might reach other rooms in the apartment, just as the conversation had reached me.

After getting out of the bath and putting on my clothes, I returned to the bathroom. I climbed onto the edge of the bathtub and shouted as loudly as I could into the vent, which was the size of two stacked paperback books.

"Is anyone there? Can you hear me? I'm being held captive here! Please call the police!"

Suddenly, someone grabbed me from behind by the clothes and pulled me down to the tile floor with immense force. It was Miyamura. Still gripping my collar, he dragged me out of the bathroom. I grabbed anything I could as I was dragged, but everything I touched was pulled along with me. Although Miyamura was shorter than me, his build was solid, and his strength was more than I had imagined. As I was dragged, I grabbed onto something else. A kitchen appliance was knocked over, crashing to the floor with a tremendous noise. My attempts to resist were in vain, and I was eventually dragged back into my room.

In a fit of anger, I slammed my fists onto the low table and bellowed at Miyamura, "Stop messing around! Let me out of here!"

Miyamura muttered, "This one's hopeless," and left the room.

For more than a month after that, I used every ounce of strength I had to try to escape. But I never managed to get out of Room 804, and no one came to help. My brother stationed himself in the small room beyond the kitchen to keep an eye on me, and the wooden door between the entrance and the Western-style room was locked tightly.

Not only were these obstacles insurmountable, but I was also painfully reminded of how much my physical strength had deteriorated over the five years and five months of confinement during the battle with my brother, sister, and mother. Despite praying to God and swearing to fight, I found that even the will to pray was fading before me. Coming to terms with this reality became incredibly painful. The fear of losing myself and possibly losing my sanity took over. I lost all the will to protest and gave up trying to escape by force.

I closed the sliding doors between my room and the kitchen so I wouldn't have to see my family or speak to them. This was the bitter conclusion of our battle.

Hunger Strike Beginning at Forty

Perhaps out of guilt, or perhaps because they didn't want to cause any more trouble, my family brought me new items: a videotape, headphones, and a desk lamp. When I asked for books I wanted to read, they brought those as well. The first book they gave me was Samuel Huntington's *The Clash of Civilizations and the Remaking of*

World Order. To escape the unbearable reality of being kidnapped, with no idea when I would be freed, I devoured the books. I could also close the sliding doors, and with the headphones, I started watching TV and recording shows I liked on videotapes.

Though reading books and watching TV helped me temporarily forget the harsh reality, it didn't clear my frustration. In fact, I often found myself more lost, wasting hours in a daze. If I hadn't been confined, I would have been building a life with my fiancée, raising children, and living a modest, happy life. The thought of that filled me with deep regret and emptiness.

Realizing how desperate my situation was, I not only wanted to keep my mind stable but also do something meaningful, not waste my time. So, I summarized the contents of the *Divine Principle* in diagrams and notes, practicing my lectures. As I watched my notebooks fill up, I convinced myself I wasn't wasting my time.

In November 2003, I faintly heard the voice of a speaker calling out, "To the residents of Ogikubo 3-chome, this is Nobuteru Ishihara speaking" from outside. This was the moment when I finally learned my location. I had longed to know where I was for the past six years, ever since my place had been moved to Room 804.

I saw on TV that the general election for the 43rd House of Representatives of Japan was to be held soon. Not only was I shocked to learn that this was Ogikubo 3-chome, but I was also filled with resentment over not being able to exercise my voting rights for eight years. How many ballots had been sent to my resident address, and how many more would be sent in the future?

Although I had given up on escaping by force, it was around

this time that I came up with the idea of an "SOS paper." I tore a page from my notebook and wrote this message with a pen:

"I am Toru Goto. I am being held captive on the upper floors of this building. If you find this paper, please contact the Unification Church. I will offer a reward."

But when I tried to drop the note to the ground, it wasn't easy. The glass window with a metal wire frame wasn't going to break easily. Even if I managed to drop the note, I didn't know what kind of punishment I would face if my family or Miyamura found out. After hesitating, I tore the paper into small pieces and flushed it down the toilet.

Three years had passed since I resorted to force, and eight years had already passed since I was kidnapped. In 2004, I turned forty years old.

For the past three years, I spent most of the time in my room, only leaving to use the bathroom. I ate the meals my mother and sister prepared alone and slept alone at night. I even started cutting my own hair with borrowed scissors. I avoided using the air conditioner because I felt the silent pressure from my family, who seemed to think I didn't deserve to use it. During winter, I wore layers of clothes to stay warm.

Whenever I wanted to read a book, I would ask my brother to bring it for me.

Books like *An Inquiry into the Good*, *The Communist Manifesto*, *Socialism: Utopian and Scientific*, *The Protestant Ethic and the Spirit of*

Capitalism, On War, The History of the People, The Morality of the People, Also sprach Zarathustra, Representative Men of Japan, Bushido, Christianity Through the Centuries, and others were brought to me. I read fifty to sixty books in total. In addition to the *Divine Principle,* I also summarized the representative texts, which explained the church's doctrine like *Essentials of Unification Thought* and *The End of Communism* in notebooks. These notebooks eventually totaled over 100 volumes.

Father in Heaven, what should I do?

There once was a time when I prayed, I felt my prayers were being answered. But now, no matter how much I prayed, I no longer received clear responses. I even began to wonder if it was God's will for me to end my life here. The God I believed in, as taught by the Unification Church, was not one who granted every wish. Though God is the omnipotent Creator, He could not help unless humans made the greatest possible efforts.

What could I do in this environment? I prayed as I thought.

To avoid getting sick, I did simple exercises in my room, but the deterioration in my physical strength was noticeable. Thanks to my efforts to brush my teeth, the only blessing was that I didn't get any cavities.

Was there any form of protest I could do, given my lack of physical strength?

The only thing left was to protest my captivity with a hunger strike.

Having reached the age of forty and entered a state of some resignation, I began to consider such an idea.

I had done fasting during my student years when I was feeling ephemeral and nihilistic, and searching for mental training. Even after joining the Unification Church, I fasted for religious purposes. Both times, it was a weeklong fast with only water, and even for just one week, the suffering from hunger was intense. Also in both cases, I had people supporting me, so the fasting was spiritually fulfilling.

However, the hunger strike I was about to attempt had a completely different purpose and environment. Although my family was around me, they were the ones who had kept me captive for years in an attempt to make me renounce my faith. I couldn't do this with anything less than full commitment. It demanded a life-or-death decision.

When the physical confrontations had continued for three years, my sister-in-law, who had been sick and staying at home, returned to monitor me in Room 804.

When my sister-in-law came back, she complained about the inconvenience of having to carry food from the kitchen to the living room. She suggested that we eat in my room again, like before. It wasn't as if the house was that large; carrying the food wasn't difficult. I could tell she didn't like the fact I was eating alone in the closed-off room.

"No," I immediately refused. "When you were gone, we discussed it, and I decided to eat by myself."

"You think you can just keep being selfish like that?"

Her voice grew harsh as she became irritated.

My sister came in, looking confused. My sister-in-law, without a word, began preparing the meal at the low table. Seeing this as an opportunity, I declared to both of them: "Fine. I won't eat. I'm going on a hunger strike to protest the confinement."

My mother, who had been in the kitchen, peeked into the room and said worriedly, "That's no use. Stop it."

I made up my mind and replied, "This is a protest against the confinement. I'll stop the hunger strike once I'm freed."

My sister asked, seemingly to confirm, "You really don't want us to prepare anything?"

"Yeah, I won't eat."

My sister-in-law, exasperated, said, "Mother, let's just leave him be. He said he's not going to eat."

From that day on, my family started eating meals in my room again.

At mealtime, I would sit in front of the closet where I usually sat, hugging my knees, while I watched them eat around the low table. It made me so angry.

"It's been eight years. The people born back then are already eight years old. They're in third grade now. This confinement is a violation of human rights," I said.

I let all my frustrations pour out, one after another.

"My thirties should have been the prime of my life, when I had the most energy and strength. But instead, I've been isolated from society and locked up here, having those years completely stolen from me. What are you going to do about that?!"

"How many times do you think my right to vote has been taken away?"

"To not see this as a violation of human rights means your thinking is seriously warped. How can you not get that? It's completely absurd."

It seemed that my family also had things they wanted to say. My mother, sister, and sister-in-law often came into the room to complain. My sister-in-law was usually the one leading the others into the room.

On the third day of my hunger strike, my sister-in-law stood in front of me alone.

"You're still not listening to anyone, huh? You really need to think for yourself," she said.

"What are you talking about? This level of human rights violation has never been seen before," I snapped back.

Her face quickly twisted into an expression of anger.

"Human rights, human rights... People like you, with rotten hearts, don't deserve any human rights!"

It wasn't unusual for her face to change drastically with rage, and she would often slap me in her fury. There was even a time when she slapped my cheek while sitting right in front of me. My sister-in-law was muscular from her swimming background, and her strikes, full of strength, left my face bruised and numb. She also seemed to hurt her hand from hitting too hard, as she used to have a patch on her thumb.

After dinner one night, my sister-in-law became hysterical while complaining in front of me. She shouted, "Get a grip!" and stormed off to the kitchen.

I could hear the loud terrifying noises from the kitchen—throwing things, objects crashing, and the sound of running water. I froze in fear, and when she returned, she was holding a large stainless bowl. Standing right in front of me, she suddenly poured its contents over my back, from my collar to my spine.

It was ice water. The cold water and ice poured into my clothes, making me shiver even more, adding to the discomfort of my fasting body. But what was even worse than the cold was the misery of being drenched in wet clothes.

The "ice water incident" was just one example of my sister-in-law's agitated behavior. Perhaps she thought it was her responsibility to be tough on me because she was someone who wasn't related by blood. Or maybe, after sacrificing her marriage and spending eight years monitoring us in the apartment, she resented me for not appreciating it. Whatever the reason, it felt like an unjust and cruel outburst of misplaced anger.

Her emotional attacks went beyond words. In the confinement, where there was no escape, her wild actions were terrifying. The hunger and physical exhaustion from the hunger strike, combined with her mistreatment, pushed me to the edge mentally. I became terrified at the mere thought of her. If I felt her presence nearby, my heart would race and my body would tense up.

Two weeks into the hunger strike, I could barely stand. I had entered uncharted territory and began to fear what might happen next. My family showed no signs of changing, and their indifference only deepened my sense of dread.

I could no longer walk, and even the smallest movements became difficult. As a result, I spent more time lying down. Not only could I no longer take a bath but even going to the bathroom became a challenge—I couldn't even stand to relieve myself. My cheeks had sunken, my ribs stuck out, and my limbs had grown even thinner. Yet, my family showed no concern. I realized that even if I continued the hunger strike, nothing would change.

On the twenty-first day, I decided to stop my hunger strike.

"I've decided to end the fast," I told my family. The next day, they prepared a meal as if nothing had happened. However, the food was easy on my stomach, as we all knew that I had to gradually ease back into eating regular food. My first meal was a watery porridge, suitable for the sick or infants. Over the next month, I was slowly transitioned from the porridge to solid foods.

In April 2005, one year later, my weakened body began to recover, so I decided to begin another hunger strike to protest my confinement. However, just like the first time, my family showed no signs of concern. As a result, I ended the second hunger strike again after three weeks. I was allowed to start eating again, but the food was still porridge, and after a month, I had not yet returned to regular meals.

By the time three months had passed and summer arrived, my meals still consisted only of porridge with miso soup, and I continued to struggle with hunger.

"I was back to regular meals in a month last time," I said. "Why is it taking so long now? Is this some kind of starvation tactic? A punishment? When will I return to regular food?"

Sensing the malice in my family's actions, I confronted my sister-in-law.

"How would I know when it will go back to normal?" she said.

It wasn't until November that I was finally given the same food as the rest of the family. The food punishment of 2005 had lasted for seven months.

In April 2006, a year later, I began my third hunger strike, this time with the intention of continuing until I was freed from my confinement. When I told my family about the hunger strike, they didn't say anything but simply left me to do as I wished.

Two weeks into the hunger strike, standing had become difficult. I struggled to read or think clearly, and spent most of the day lying down. By the time I reached three weeks, I was overwhelmed by an unfamiliar pain, my awareness began to fade, and my breathing became shallow.

My mother finally became concerned and said, "Why don't you end it now?" But even after several more days, my family still refused to end the confinement.

I truly felt I might die. I even wondered if dying here was God's will. As my consciousness blurred, I couldn't pray anymore. Yet, the closer death seemed, the stronger my will to survive became. I couldn't die now.

One day, I quietly told my family, "I'm ending the hunger strike." It had been thirty days since I stopped eating.

The food should have started with porridge and gradually transitioned back to regular meals. But an entire day passed without any porridge being served.

Are they trying to kill me?

For the first time, my family looked tense, their faces stiff with unease.

It was my sister-in-law's voice that shattered the cold silence. "What are you talking about? You fasted on your own, and now you're asking for food?"

My sister followed up with a harsh comment, "Are you crazy?"

Without missing a beat, my sister-in-law added, "Keep fasting until you die."

I could not shake the feeling that I might die. Despite my determination to go on a hunger strike, the fear of death made my resolve weaken. In desperation, I humbly begged my family to give me food.

The next day, breakfast was served, and I felt a sense of relief, thinking, *At least I won't die now*. But when I looked at what was placed before me, I could not believe my eyes: It was a small dish, almost like an appetizer. It was a tiny bowl, barely wider than my index finger and only as deep as my little finger, filled about three-quarters with watery porridge. Until the last hunger strike, porridge had always been served in a regular soup bowl.

I didn't want to watch my family eat, so I turned to face the wall and began eating my porridge.

"Hey, turn this way!" My sister-in-law shouted angrily, banging the table. "Sit here!" she ordered. I didn't understand why, but I feared they would take the porridge away if I didn't follow her orders, so I sat where I was told.

For both lunch and dinner, I was served the same tiny portion of watery porridge. During the day, I was given diluted sports drinks, 500 milliliters twice a day. This was the first meal after my hunger strike ended.

For five more days, nothing changed. The same small dish was placed in front of me, and I sipped the porridge slowly, watching my family eat. The meal only lasted about three minutes, leaving me hungry and miserable.

Since this fast had been nine days longer than the two before, I thought it would take time to return to regular meals—starting with watery porridge, then regular porridge, and eventually normal food. I tried to convince myself to endure it. Honestly, though, I desperately wanted to eat more. I wished they would speed up the process of getting back to normal meals. But with my mother, brother, sister-in-law, and sister eating silently with stern faces, I totally couldn't bring myself to ask.

Ten days after my thirty-day hunger strike ended, the tiny portion of watery porridge was still the same. My body had become emaciated, and I looked like a person on the verge of starvation.

It was a form of food punishment. It could only be done intentionally.

By giving me only a watery porridge and sports drinks, it was like I wasn't eating at all. After enduring thirty days of a hunger strike, I was forced into another ten days of near-fasting, and I found myself facing the fear of starving to death.

I would be killed by hunger.

To survive, I started looking for anything I could put in my mouth.

There was a refrigerator behind the sliding door in my room. I quietly opened it, and in the dim light, I saw food inside. My hunger made my mouth water, but I knew if I got caught stealing food, the punishment would be severe. My hunger made it hard to think clearly, but I tried desperately to come up with an idea.

I found sauces like mayonnaise and ketchup in the door pocket. I cautiously took out the mayonnaise, opened the cap, and squeezed some into my hand. I went back to my room and slowly licked the mayonnaise. Even though I knew the strong taste would be harsh on my weakened stomach, I couldn't think about that.

From then on, I secretly ate mayonnaise, ketchup, and Worcestershire sauce to curb my hunger. But about a week later, the condiments were completely gone from the fridge. When did they find out I was sneaking food? I had to do something or I would really die.

I was allowed to drink water at the kitchen sink. I used water repeatedly to dull my hunger and noticed there were scraps of food in the corner of the sink. I felt an overwhelming urge to eat them all, but if they were gone too quickly, I would be caught. So, I decided to secretly take some carrot peels, apple skins, and cabbage cores, one by one, and eat them in my room.

From that day on, I became hyper-aware of every sound my mother and sister made while cooking in the kitchen. From the sound of the knife on the cutting board, I could imagine what vegetables and fruits they were preparing, and I felt euphoric just thinking about the scraps they would throw away. Once they finished their meal, I couldn't wait to get to the kitchen and check what scraps were left in the sink. Especially, if there were apple peels, my heart would race. I would carefully take them, return to my room, cut them into small pieces, and savor them. The little bits of fruit still clinging to the peel released a burst of sweetness in my mouth, and I cried from how delicious it was.

But after a while, the scraps in the sink disappeared.

When did they find out? Since it had been a long time since I had spoken to my family, it was too terrifying to ask them.

Forty days had passed since I finished my thirty-day fast. My only food was still a small bowl of watery porridge and a sports drink. At this rate, I didn't think I would survive. I had managed to survive on seasonings and food waste, but I felt as if even God had abandoned me.

Between Life and Death

Due to the hunger, I had become completely unable to do anything. I couldn't read books or newspapers, nor could I watch television. I was in a semiconscious condition, and I spent the entire day lying down.

As I stared at the cloudy glass, tinted orange by the sunset, I suddenly heard some music. The sound was like a harp, and the melody felt familiar and nostalgic. It was so beautiful and surreal that for a brief moment, I completely forgot about my hunger.

Where was this music coming from?

It wasn't the children's song, *Yuyake Koyake* (Sunset), that plays from the speakers in Suginami.

There was no place around here that would play such music.

It was a hallucination.

Or, maybe it was a call from the other side. A deep sense of gratitude toward the God who had kept me alive filled me, and tears began to flow. I was ready to die.

After a while, I heard someone preparing dinner in the kitchen. I recognized the sound of rice being washed, and it felt like a glimmer of hope. The rice, now washed, was placed in a bowl with water and left to soak in the sink for about thirty minutes to an hour. At that moment, no one was in the kitchen. I had thought that raw rice would be too hard to eat, but I had no choice but to try.

Once the kitchen fell silent, I seized the chance, opened the sliding door, and made my way to the sink. Carefully, I picked up a little soaked rice from the bowl with my fingers and returned to my room, sitting down on the tatami mat. The rice, now white from soaking in water, was in my hand. I took five grains, put them in my mouth, and chewed them with my back teeth. To my surprise, they were soft, and as I chewed, a roasted flavor spread across my mouth.

"Delicious," I whispered to myself.

I had become hooked on the soaked raw rice.

With the condiments gone from the fridge and the scraps in the sink no longer available, raw rice was the only thing I could eat.

It was my last lifeline. If the raw rice was hidden from me, it would be the end.

So, my secret ritual of stealing raw rice began.

Two hours before each meal, either my mother or sister would wash the rice. When I heard the rhythmic sound of rice washing in the kitchen, my heart would race with anticipation. After about twenty minutes, when the rice had soaked, I would go to the bathroom. Once I came out, I'd pretend to wash my hands at the sink. Then, I would sneak a little raw rice and return to my room to eat it, savoring each grain. The roasted taste spread in my mouth. It was my blissful moment.

The unbearable hunger and the surprising taste of the raw rice slowly made me bolder, and I began taking more from the bowl. Eventually, I think I was taking nearly half a cup of rice.

When cooking rice, if too much water is added, the texture of the cooked rice changes.

At the dinner table, my brother commented, "The rice has been softer lately." My mother and sister nodded in agreement, saying, "Yeah, that's strange." My sister-in-law looked uneasy, staring at her bowl with a displeased expression.

I was quietly sipping the watery porridge from my small bowl. Inside, I was silently pleading, "God, please help me not get caught!" I felt like I was walking a tightrope.

But despite my fear, I couldn't stop stealing the raw rice. The days went on with the rice always turning out too soft and watery.

"The rice cooker is broken," my brother said.

"It can't be helped," my mother and sister replied, sounding disappointed.

Soon, the old rice cooker was replaced with a new one. My family mistakenly thought it had started to malfunction. Amazingly, no one figured out that I had been secretly taking and eating the raw rice. It felt like a miracle.

However, this didn't do anything to ease my hunger. I remembered reading an article in the *Sankei* newspaper that mentioned the tragic deaths of several young Irish revolutionaries, who died in the 1980s after fasting for forty to seventy days. I thought that after fasting for thirty days, and surviving on only watery porridge and sports drinks, eating only small amounts of raw rice would still ultimately lead to starvation, just like those young revolutionaries.

It had been seventy days since I stopped my hunger strike on July 10, 2006. I gathered my courage and said, "I can't go on like this. Please, I'm begging you, let me eat regular food."

My brother paused for a moment, then replied, "Maybe it's time to go back to normal."

"Eh, really?" my sister-in-law said.

I froze at the disappointed tone in her voice.

From that day on, the small porridge bowl was replaced with a regular soup bowl. The porridge increased in quantity and even had a few grains of rice mixed in. Finally, I felt a sense of relief, thinking that I might survive after all.

The porridge gradually changed from thin rice porridge to thicker versions, and after four months, I was finally given regular cooked rice.

The first meal was as follows:

Breakfast: One slice of bread, with a drink

Lunch: One bowl of rice, miso soup, a small dish of nori (seaweed), pickled vegetables, a little fish, and umeboshi (pickled plum)

Dinner: One bowl of rice, miso soup, pickled vegetables, small shrimp, and natto (fermented soybeans)

My side dishes were served on small plates, about the size of a postcard. I had hoped I would eventually be able to eat the same food as the rest of my family, but the reality wasn't so simple.

A month passed, then six months, and even a year later, my meals, portions, and small plates stayed the same. Meanwhile, my family was eating curry rice, dumplings, katsudon (pork cutlet rice bowl), ramen, croquettes, tempura, grilled fish, and more—all at the same table as me.

I longed to eat what they were having in front of me, but I couldn't bring myself to ask, "Why am I still eating differently?" I was terrified of asking, afraid that if I upset them, my portion would be reduced even more.

What bothered me the most during this time were the days when curry was served at the table. The smell of curry in front of me only made my hunger worse. On those nights, the family would save the leftover curry sauce to use the next day for curry udon. This "curry hell" lasted two days each time.

But that wasn't all. After lunch, my family would always have yogurt with seasonal fruits, and I could only watch helplessly. After the meal, they would enjoy desserts like sweets and fruits in another room. Due to my hunger, I became so sensitive to smells that I could easily tell what kind of desserts they were eating—apples, oranges, chocolate, or cookies. Drawn in by the sweet scents, I ended up going through the leftover scraps in the kitchen, but all I could find were apple peels.

My body—now nothing but skin and bones—never seemed to recover. The constant hunger tormented me, and even when I lay in bed, I couldn't sleep. My mind would flood with images of the foods I craved—curry, katsudon, anpan (sweet red bean buns), and various fruits. I couldn't sleep from the hunger.

Love Your Enemies

In 2006, with its thirty-day hunger strike and months of harsh food punishment, the confinement period surpassed ten years, and I was about to enter the eleventh year.

At some point in 2005, the newspaper I had been receiving switched from *Sankei Shimbun* to *Tokyo Shimbun*, but by June 2006, even the *Tokyo Shimbun* stopped being delivered to my room. Weakened and hungry, I started to hear a beautiful melody in my hallucinations—while I was trying to survive by secretly eating scraps and raw rice. My consciousness was fading, and I spent most of the day either lying down or propped up against the wall. I no longer had the strength to read the newspaper, so maybe my family thought it wasn't necessary to deliver it anymore.

In September, three months after I stopped reading the newspaper, my sister was cleaning my room, and, without asking me, she picked up a videotape I had been using to record a program.

"Don't take that, I'm still using it," I said, attempting to grab the tape from her hand. She refused to let go, and with an unpleasant sound, the tape casing broke.

"Hey, why did you break it?"

"You wouldn't let go," she replied.

It turned into an argument.

Then my sister-in-law came in, pulled the antenna cable plugged into the wall and disconnected it from the TV as well. Not a word was spoken. After that, when I tried to turn on the TV, all I saw was static.

Just like at the start of my confinement, I was no longer able to watch TV or read a newspaper. Once again, I had lost all means of connecting to the outside world. For me, time had stopped with the news of the birth of the Shinzo Abe administration.

Even then, I couldn't oppose the actions of my sister and sister-in-law.

What I feared most was that my food rations would be cut even further. My anger at my family's unreasonable actions was over-shadowed by the much greater fear of upsetting them and facing even harsher food restrictions. Even though I could no longer read the newspaper or watch TV, I had to monitor my family's expressions closely, out of fear of hunger.

I had lost so much weight. Before I was confined, I was 182 cm tall and weighed around 65 kg. But now, I felt like I had dropped to about 45 kg. My muscles had wasted away, my ribs were sticking out, and my arms and legs were unnaturally thin. When I struggled with my sister over the videotape, I had no strength to fight back, and when my sister-in-law took the TV antenna cable, I could only watch helplessly.

One of the core teachings of the Unification Church is "Love your enemies." This teaching emphasizes a high level of love, where you must love even those who persecute you, without harboring any hatred or seeking revenge. In the New Testament, Jesus Christ also teaches, "Love your enemies and pray for those who persecute you."

During my confinement, I constantly kept this teaching in mind. Since kidnapping and confinement are crimes, I harshly criticized my family for what they were doing. At times, we had intense clashes. But in my heart, I made efforts to remove hatred and resentment by praying. I applied the same mindset toward Miyamura and the former believers. However, this wasn't easy—it was a constant "battle with myself." That's why, despite protesting and resisting the confinement, I never resorted to violence. I truly believe that the reason my mind didn't break completely was because of my efforts and the "divine protection" I felt.

But after ten years of confinement, I found myself unable to control the growing feelings of hatred.

What my mother, brother, sister, and sister-in-law had done, I believed, was because they truly thought it was for my own good—that they were acting in my best interest. However, over the years, they had changed completely. The influence of Miyamura on them must have been too strong. I felt that they no longer saw me as part of the family but as a dangerous person, tainted by the *Divine Principle*, whose poison could never be removed. As the confinement dragged on, the more they sacrificed their own lives, and it seemed that their accumulated frustrations were now being directed at me.

Even considering all the circumstances, ten years was far too long. What right did my family have to strip me of my freedom for that long? And to make matters worse, they didn't even provide me with proper meals. I was hungry all the time, my body had withered away, and I could no longer even protest. Day after day, at mealtimes, there was one thing placed only in front of me—a small dish of pickled plum. The family had sat expressionless, with faces like Noh masks.

But that wasn't all. To me, my brother, his wife, and my sister were "traitors" to the faith. They had spoken ill of and mocked Reverend Moon, whom I revere as the Messiah. Their words and actions were unforgivable.

As the days passed, resentment slowly took root deep in my heart, and it began to fester and rot. Even though I kept praying, telling myself to "love your enemies" and trying to rid myself of the resentment, I couldn't. It felt like talking to a brick wall. I feared that if this confinement continued, the dam inside me would break, and I would give in to the whispers of darkness, eventually leading to self-harm or harming others.

The growing resentment seemed beyond my control. The only way to cleanse this rising bitterness was to rely on God. I had no choice but to cling to Him, knowing He understood everything I was going through. All I could do was pray.

However, after ten years of confinement, there were moments when I felt abandoned by God. I often fell into despair, wondering if this would be my life forever.

Although I had been blessed through prayer in the past, I now felt as though I had hit a wall. I knew I needed to devote myself to prayer more than ever before. I started to integrate longer prayer sessions into my daily routine.

The best time for me to pray, when I could fully focus, was early in the morning before the family woke up. I spent two to three hours each morning solely on prayer. It was the first time I had ever committed so much time to prayer every day.

In December 2006, I began my early morning prayers.

On the first day, I woke up while it was still dark. It actually worked out that I had been waking up in the middle of the night from hunger. The way I had arranged my futon against the wall also turned out to be ideal, as it allowed me to sit cross-legged and pray, with the wall providing support behind me.

I shivered from the cool wall. As I couldn't use the heating function on the air conditioner in my room, sensing the silent pressure from my family, I wrapped the blanket around my shoulders to keep warm. If anyone had seen me, it would have looked like only my face was visible, with the futon pressed up against the wall.

The prayer sessions were from 4:00 a.m. to 7:00 a.m.

"Heavenly Father, it's been ten years since I was confined. I don't know how much longer I can bear this. I can't suppress my hatred. What should I do?" I prayed earnestly.

At first, hunger distracted me during the morning prayers, and all I could think about was food. Time just passed, and all I was left with was a sense of exhaustion. On top of that, an overwhelming darkness seemed to press down on me, as though it were blocking my prayers from reaching God.

After a month of praying, I began to feel some response. I sensed intuitively that I was loved by God, and an indescribable sense of peace filled me. While I'm not sure if this idea would resonate with those of different faiths or those without any faith, the heavy darkness that had surrounded me slowly lifted, and I felt a warm light enveloping me. There seemed to be a clear, straight path of light extending from my back up to the heavens.

God's message came to me as a voice and as inspiration:

Trust in Me. I will lead you. Surrender to Me.

Watch closely. My power. My work.

These internal messages made me feel certain that God had not abandoned me. I decided to write down the repeated messages, believing that they were the most important things God wanted to tell me.

Since spring, my family had stopped providing me with writing materials, like notebooks and pens. Since being moved to Room 804, I had to use an old calendar I kept in the closet for when I would run out of notebooks. Having used up all the ballpoint pens, I resorted to a mechanical pencil with only a few leads left. Both the calendar and the pencil leads were precious and limited, so I wrote as small as possible to make them last longer.

In the darkness, I would wait for dawn's light to begin writing down the messages. Whenever I received a repeated message, I would add a mark of plus signs on the right side of the words.

I received this message frequently:

The more opposition and persecution intensify, the less you lose; sins will be cleansed faster, and restitution will inevitably be required. The opponents will be forced to make restitution.

I interpreted it as a religious perspective on "persecution." I believed that suffering and hardship, when accepted with the right heart, would instead clear one's debts, and that the persecutors would ultimately be the ones responsible for restitution.

The calendar was soon filled with messages from God.

Four months passed, and by April 2007, the cold had eased, and I no longer needed the blanket to pray. Yet, my heart was still burdened with lingering feelings of resentment.

I began receiving words like this:

Still, I love them. I want to save them. This is My heart. As their Messiah, love them, love them, love them, and save them. Save them. Don't hesitate. Love and save them.

I was deeply moved by God's immense, unconditional love, and tears flowed uncontrollably.

Before going to bed, I started cutting a square of toilet paper about fifty centimeters long and folding it into smaller squares—around six or seven of them—which I would place by my pillow for the night. The next morning, as I prayed, God's emotions overwhelmed me, and tears and snot flowed. Then I would pull out a folded piece of toilet paper from under the blanket and wipe my tears and nose. By the time the prayer session ended, I had usually used up all the tissues I had prepared. All that was left were gray, crumpled balls of paper, soaked with my tears and snot.

Another important message was:

It will definitely fall. Make miracles. When the time comes, I will guide you. Even the Roman Empire, which persecuted Christianity, eventually fell. It is destined to fall. Even if it seems impossible, if the conditions are fulfilled, it will definitely fall.

I interpreted this message as one of hope, much like how Christianity, despite persecution by the Roman Empire, eventually became the state religion. It meant that if the right conditions were met, there would come a time when I would finally be able to leave this building.

Standing on the edge of despair, I began to see a faint glimmer of hope through the spiritual strength, comfort, and powerful revelations I received in my prayers.

Heading to the Shoto Headquarters

February 10, 2008, was a Sunday. One year had passed since I began my early morning prayers. In Room 804, which was inside a thick concrete building, the cold was so intense it seemed to pierce through to my bones.

Around 4:00 p.m., when the daylight began to fade, my brother and his wife, my mother, and my sister entered my room. They all sat in a row in front of me, their expressions stern.

My brother spoke first.

"What do you want? Don't you want to think about whether the Unification Church is really correct?"

"I have no intention of reviewing anything in this confinement room."

Everyone went quiet and stayed still.

"Are you sure that's how you feel?"

"Yes. Don't make me say it again."

My brother glared at me and said more firmly, "Then leave."

For a moment, I couldn't comprehend what my brother was saying. The one who had been preventing my escape with force was now telling me to leave? What did he think my life was?

"Then at least give me some money. I can't even take the train without it," I said.

When I was abducted from my parents' house, I had around 10,000 yen in my wallet. But I had left it behind at the apartment in Niigata, and they never gave me back my wallet or the money.

"No. I'm not giving you any money."

My brother's response must have reflected the family's consensus.

I was thirty-one years old when I was abducted. Now, I was forty-four. Despite having my precious time and all my opportunities taken from me, was I supposed to be thrown out with nothing, just the clothes on my back, because I didn't agree with the family's wishes? Wasn't this treatment utterly unreasonable?

"Locking me up for twelve years and then kicking me out without a penny is just cruel. This is ridiculous!"

The moment I shouted in anger, my brother suddenly became

furious and lunged at me. Not only my brother but also my sister-in-law and even my mother grabbed me, lifting me by my arms and body, joining in to overpower me. Though I tried to resist, my weak, emaciated body was no match for them. I was carried out through the front door and thrown onto the cold concrete hallway. As I lay there on my back, unable to get up, my brother yelled, "Shoes! Shoes!" and someone threw a pair of leather shoes at me. In an instant, the front door slammed shut, and I heard the sound of the lock turning.

I was bleeding from my knuckles and wrists, and my sweater was torn.

"Don't mess with me!" Furious at how I had been treated, I kept banging on the door and protesting.

"Shut up!" my brother yelled from behind the door.

I came to my senses and realized that, just as I had hoped, I had been set free.

Stunned, I put on the leather shoes that had been thrown at me and took the elevator down to the first floor. When I stepped outside through the entrance, the sunlight before dusk illuminated the streets of Ogikubo. I looked up at the sky, and it was a clear, wintry sky. People and cars were passing by.

Surrounded by the cool air, I took a deep breath.

I was free.

Like the ice in the shaded areas slowly melting under the sun, a sense of liberation gradually rose within me. When I looked back, I saw the nameplate "Flower Mansion" in cut letters above the entrance. It was the first time I had known the name of the building I had been confined in for ten years.

I did it. Now I was free. After twelve years and five months, I had been released from my captivity.

However, the joy lasted only a moment. I was brought back to the harsh reality of being weak, penniless, no destination, and starving. As I looked at a utility pole to write down the address of the building, I saw the number for Ogikubo in Suginami Ward. I scratched the number onto the back of a discarded flyer using a small stone I picked up from a potted plant on the sidewalk.

The sun was setting, and in about an hour, it would be dark. I had no choice but to return to the Unification Church and explain my situation. But I didn't know where any of its facilities were near Ogikubo. If I went to the Shoto headquarters in Shibuya, I figured I could manage. I folded the flyer with the address of the apartment and put it in the pocket of my sweatpants. I then headed toward the Unification Church headquarters.

As I walked a little further down the main road in front of the apartment, I realized it was the Ome-kaido Avenue. I knew that the Ome-kaido crossed Tokyo from west to east, so I decided to head east for now. After a while, I came across a sign for the "Narimune Police Box."

I decided to report the confinement to the police. I thought they would surely help me.

I opened the door of the police box, where two officers were sitting. "Excuse me," I said. "I was confined at a place called 'Flower Mansion' nearby, and I was just released."

The two officers stood up in surprise, studying me closely. My appearance, as someone who had just been suddenly kicked out of an apartment with no belongings, was disheveled. I was wearing a faded, worn-out, red-striped sweater with a tear on the side; black sweatpants; old shoes with tassels; and a self-cut, unkempt hairstyle. Nothing about me looked normal.

One of the officers quietly closed the sliding door behind me and asked, "Can you tell us more about what happened?"

I explained that I was a member of the Unification Church, that my family had kidnapped and confined me to make me renounce my faith, and that I had been held captive for twelve years. The two officers listened attentively, but gradually their expressions grew more confused.

"I see. But your family was with you, right?"

"Yes."

"And you were eating food, right?"

"Yes, I was eating."

Then, with an apologetic tone, the officer said, "Well, in that case, there's not much we can do."

"But I was confined!" I said, raising my voice, but the officer responded, "Your parents were with you, right?"

It felt like the conversation was going nowhere.

At least I wanted to borrow some money for train fare.

"I don't have any money on me, so could you lend me some money?"

The officer then asked, "What's your current address?" "Do you have any ID?" "Do you have any friends in Tokyo?"

I replied, "No, I was locked up in an apartment for twelve years.

I just got out, and I have nothing with me, no place to go."

"Well, that makes things a bit difficult."

They refused to lend me even train fare because they didn't know who I was. I was left speechless.

I had no choice but to walk to the headquarters. I asked the officer for directions to Shibuya.

"You're walking to Shibuya?"

"Yes. How far is it?"

"Well, it's quite far."

"Can I walk there?"

"Well, it's not impossible."

One of the officers took out a piece of paper and, with a pencil, drew a simple map to show me the directions.

"Stay on Ome-kaido Avenue heading east, and when you reach the intersection with Meiji Street, turn right. Then head south on Meiji Street. You'll see 'Nakano-Sakaue' subway station at the next intersection. This is the simplest way.

It seemed that the headquarters in Shibuya was about ten kilometers away. Holding the piece of paper with the directions, I left the police box. It was already growing dim outside. I felt a sense of urgency. If I didn't get to the headquarters soon, it would be closing time.

Later, it occurred to me that the officers probably hadn't noticed how much weight I had lost. Due to the silent pressure from my family, who had been questioning whether I had the right to use the room heater, I had layered my clothes heavily. I was wearing eight layers on my upper body—short-sleeved shirts, two long-sleeved shirts, two sweatshirts, and three sweaters—along with three layers on my lower body, including a pair of pants and two pairs of tracksuit bottoms. If I had taken off my clothes in front of the officers and revealed my emaciated body, perhaps they would have reacted differently.

After twelve years and five months, walking freely on my own feet was an incredibly exciting experience. Although the physical damage from the confinement was significant, and there were days when I couldn't exercise, I was able to walk relatively fast, perhaps because I had made an effort to keep my body moving.

As I walked along the sidewalk, I encountered all sorts of people: a middle-aged woman with a grocery bag, a young couple holding hands with their little girl, and a young man speeding by on a bicycle. Having been confined for twelve years in a small room on the eighth floor, seeing people walking past me on the street felt like such a refreshing experience.

Having been deprived of proper meals for so long, I couldn't resist the delicious smells of ramen and donuts as I passed by restaurants. The urge to fill my empty stomach hit me several times, but without any money, there was nothing I could do. I kept telling myself that once I had some money, I'd head straight to an all-you-can-eat restaurant and finally eat my fill. I urged myself to push forward.

After walking for about an hour, covering around five kilometers along the ginkgo tree-lined Ome-kaido Avenue, which widened from two to three lanes, I finally reached a large intersection with Yamate Avenue. It was the Nakano-Sakaue intersection. I crossed the pedestrian crosswalk and followed the directions from the sketch on the paper, heading south along Yamate Avenue.

As I walked, the lights were beginning to glow and the familiar skyline of Shinjuku emerged in the west, bathed in the warm glow of the setting sun. The skyscrapers, including the Tokyo Metropolitan Government Building, brought a sense of nostalgia and joy. A smile spread across my face as I felt the real sense of liberation after being freed from my confinement.

But an unexpected change started to happen in my body. The muscles below my knees began to gradually ache. As the pain intensified, my pace slowed. By the time I passed the intersection of Yamate Avenue and National Route 20 near the Keio Line's Hatsudai Station, the pain had escalated from simple discomfort to something much sharper. Each step sent a stabbing pain through my legs, and as I continued walking, my knees began to shake, unable to bear the pressure. It was clear that after walking such a long distance for the first time in years, my knees were beginning to buckle. I had no choice but to lean forward, placing my hands on my knees for support, and walk slowly. It had grown completely dark, and my anxiety was rising.

Would I be able to make it at this pace?

It became so difficult that I could barely stand, and I started looking for something to support my weight. There were construction sites all along Yamate Avenue, and I noticed yellow-and-black barricades with flashing red warning lights. Near one of the sites, I found a wooden pole about a meter long lying on the ground. I picked it up and found it was perfect as a walking stick. Using it for support, I slowly continued on my way.

After crossing the elevated bridge where Yamate Avenue intersects with the Odakyu Line, I reached a large intersection and spotted the pedestrian bridge over Inokashira Street.

Climbing up and then down those stairs would be too much.

I looked around for another way to cross the street without using the pedestrian bridge, but I couldn't find any signals or crosswalks. It seemed I had no choice but to use the bridge.

I gazed up at the stairs of the pedestrian bridge, illuminated by the streetlights. What would have been an easy task under normal circumstances now seemed like a monstrous obstacle blocking my way. Summoning all my determination, I stepped onto the stairs, gripping the railing to endure the sharp pain, and slowly made my way up, one step at a time. When I reached the other side and started descending, I clung to the handrail, gritting my teeth and taking each step slowly.

I had already lost a lot of time. I absolutely had to make it to the headquarters before it closed.

As I crossed the pedestrian bridge and kept walking, the pain below my knees grew worse, and I could no longer rely on the stick alone. To ease the pain, I gripped the stick with my right hand and used my left hand to support my left knee as I walked. My back hunched painfully, and my posture became awkward, but I had no choice.

On a Sunday night, the streets of Yamate Avenue were quiet, with few people around. Every now and then, passersby would glance at me with suspicion. I was dressed in a torn sweater and tracksuit, wearing leather shoes, and had a nearly shaved head with a rough, uneven haircut. On top of that, hunched over with a cane and walking unsteadily, I probably appeared to be either a homeless man or someone unusual to anyone who passed by.

After walking a bit further and passing a large intersection, I saw a utility pole with the address "Shibuya-ku, Shoto" written on it.

I had finally made it to Shoto. A sense of encouragement washed over me, and I felt a bit of strength returning.

But just after passing the pole, the pain in my knees became unbearable, and I couldn't take another step. *This is it*, I thought, sitting down on the edge of the sidewalk.

If I had a map, I would have realized that the place where I sat down was at the intersection of "Shoto 2-chome." If I had turned left and walked about 150 meters, I would have reached the Tokyu Department Store. The Unification Church headquarters was just seventy meters further. It was a distance I could have covered in fifteen minutes, if I had the strength. But in the darkness of the night, unfamiliar with the roads in Shibuya, I had no idea which way to go. The map I had gotten from the police station only showed the route south along Yamate Avenue, so it was no longer useful.

It must have been around 8:00 p.m. By that time, about four hours had passed since I left the Flower Mansion. Thankfully, I had layered my clothing, but it was the coldest time of the year, and the cold air was starting to penetrate my skin.

If I continued like this, I will fall down here and die.

I hugged my knees, curled up, and rubbed my aching legs. Twelve years and five months of captivity, filled with trials and God's guidance, flashed before my eyes like a film reel. I buried my face in my knees and prayed to God.

"Heavenly Father, I thank You for keeping and guiding me this far. I can't go any further. If it's Your will for me to end here, please let it be as You will."

As I prepared to accept my fate, a voice—without words— echoed in my heart.

Don't give up.

I raised my head.

I decided to move, even crawl, as far as I could. Clutching the stick with both hands, I gritted my teeth and forced myself to stand.

I didn't know the way. At this point, I had no choice but to ask someone passing by for directions. I hesitated, unsure about approaching anyone on this desolate street while looking like a homeless person, but I couldn't worry about that anymore.

A middle-aged man walked by, and I gathered the courage to approach him.

"Excuse me, I believe the headquarters of the Unification Church is nearby. Do you know where it is?"

He stopped in his tracks, looking surprised, and then gave me a confused look. "I live around here, but I don't know," he said, quickly walking away.

Could it be that the church headquarters had disappeared while I was confined? After twelve years and five months, anything could have happened.

After a while, a young woman walked toward me from the left side of the intersection. There were hardly any people around. I wondered if she would get scared and walk away if I spoke to her. But if I didn't ask, I might be out of options.

"Excuse me, could you tell me how to get to the headquarters of the Unification Church?"

As I asked, leaning on the stick for support, the woman seemed surprised.

"Eh?"

"Holy Spirit Association for the Unification of World Christianity," I clarified, giving the full name.

"What's happened to you?"

I was able to take a proper look at her. She was dressed in a beige trench coat and looked elegant.

"You might not believe me," I said, trying not to scare her, "I'm a member of the Unification Church. And I was kidnapped and confined twelve years ago, and today I was released. I've been walking since then."

The woman calmly took a thin black book from her bag and showed it to me. I gasped in surprise—it was unmistakably the hymnal of the Unification Church.

"I'm a Shikku too," she said.

"Shikku," meaning family, is a Korean term used affectionately among fellow church members. She was the first Unification Church member I had met in twelve years and five months.

It was Sunday, the day when Christian churches hold their services. The woman was part of a choir that sings praises to God during the services, and she was carrying a large hymnal.

Meeting a church member felt like a miracle.

I truly believed that God had brought us together. The encounter with the living God filled me with such emotion that my entire body trembled, from head to toe.

I asked the woman about something that had been on my mind throughout my years of confinement: Reverend Sun Myung Moon.

"How is Father?" I asked.

"He's doing well," she replied, her face lighting up with a warm smile.

A wave of relief and gratitude washed over me, and I thanked God deeply.

The woman then began speaking on the phone with a fellow believer. However, her expression shifted, and she seemed to be considering something carefully. It was understandable that someone might find it hard to believe that a man who was in such strange clothes and claiming to be a church member would approach them on the street.

"I actually have no money," I explained. The woman pointed back in the direction she had come from.

"If you go straight down this road and turn left, you'll reach the headquarters. Can you walk?"

The pain in my knees was so severe that it contorted my face.

"I can't walk anymore."

"Then let's get a taxi."

The woman walked to the street and raised her hand to hail a cab. A taxi appeared, its hazard lights flashing as it stopped. The back door opened, and she asked the driver, "Do you know where the Unification Church headquarters is?"

"I'm not sure," the driver replied.

The woman gave the driver directions and then said, "It's a short distance, so it should only be about a thousand yen." She took out two 500 yen coins from her wallet and handed them to him.

Before getting into the taxi, I asked, "What's your name?"

"If we're meant to meet again, we will," she replied cheerfully.

I placed the wooden stick that had supported me on the sidewalk and then, clutching my aching knees, got into the taxi. For the first time in over twelve years of confinement, I felt the warmth of human kindness. Tears of gratitude streamed down my cheeks. I bowed my head to the woman, and the taxi drove away.

The driver seemed unfamiliar with the one-way streets in Shoto, and the taxi kept circling as if it had gotten lost in a maze. After a long detour, we finally arrived at the Unification Church headquarters in Shoto 1-chome, but the fare had exceeded 1,000 yen on the meter.

"I'm sorry, I don't have any money," I said.

"Then alright," the driver replied. It seemed that he had sensed the situation from my appearance and understood.

I didn't have time to feel nostalgic about the headquarters, which I hadn't seen in so long. As soon as I stepped out of the taxi, the intense pain caused me to collapse right there. I needed to cross about five meters from the left side of the road to the entrance of the church. Placing my hands on my knees, I struggled to stand, but the constant flow of taxis heading to Shibuya Station made it hard to take a step. Gripping both knees, I moved my feet slowly, alternating between left and right, and eventually managed to cross the road.

The entrance had its shutters down, likely because it was nearing 9:00 p.m. I was prepared to sleep outside, but I decided to try the intercom, thinking it was worth a shot. After a brief pause, the shutters began to roll open with a clattering sound. Through the glass door, I saw a man.

As soon as I entered, I collapsed onto the floor in front of the reception desk. "Please, may I sit down?" I said.

"Who are you?" the security guard asked, eyeing me suspiciously, trying to figure out who I was.

I explained my twelve years and five months of captivity, but it seemed difficult for him to grasp the situation.

"Your parents are in Tokyo, right? We're having some issues here. Why don't you go back to them?"

He clearly didn't understand the situation.

The security guard looked troubled.

"I really can't stand up. Could you please help me?" I said.

Looking completely at a loss, the guard made a phone call to someone, presumably his superior, for guidance.

"Yes. He says he's been held captive for nearly thirteen years,"

I heard the guard say. Then while still on the phone, he turned to me and asked, "What's your name?"

"I'm Toru Goto."

The security guard hung up the phone.

"Someone knowledgeable about abduction and confinement is on their way. Please come inside."

It seemed I had earned his trust.

Unable to stand on my own, the security guard took my hand and helped me, guiding me to the sofa in the waiting room.

At last, I had reached the headquarters, and I felt a deep sense of relief, realizing I was finally safe.

"Have you had dinner?" the security guard asked.

"No, not yet," I replied.

"I'll go buy something for you," he said, stepping out of the waiting room. He soon returned with a plastic bag.

The table was filled with items he had bought from the convenience store.

I couldn't believe my eyes.

The foods laid out on the table were the "Best of the Menu" that I had dreamed of during the sleepless nights of hunger while I was confined—curry with a cutlet, sweet anpan (red bean buns), warm nikuman (steamed meat buns), and fruit yogurt.

The memories of the two days of "curry hell" and the resentment I had felt toward the fruit yogurt I could only watch in envy seemed to melt away all at once.

A voice, though silent, echoed in my heart.

You held up well. Now, eat as much as you want.

I thanked God and, overwhelmed with happiness, tears ran down my face as I savored each dish.

Just as I had let out a sigh of relief from the fullness, an official from the headquarters, contacted by the security guard, arrived and entered the waiting room. It was Mr. Tomohisa Ohta, the head of the public relations department at the time.

Mr. Ohta sat down in front of me and looked at me with concern.

"You really made it back," he said.

He explained that after the security guard's call, he immediately recognized who I was.

He then explained that around eleven years ago, in 1997, a particularly brutal incident of abduction and confinement occurred, known as the "Tottori Church Attack."

The victim of this incident, Ms. Hiroko Tomizawa, who was thirty-one years old at the time, was at the Tottori Church, a branch of the Unification Church. In broad daylight, a group of about a dozen people, including her father, barged in carrying stun guns, crowbars, and chains. They attacked the church staff who tried to stop them, and several men forcibly carried Ms. Tomizawa, who resisted, and shoved her into a car, abducting her.

In March 1998, Miyamura visited the apartment in Osaka where Ms. Tomizawa had been held captive, bringing two former believers from Tokyo. This coincided with the time when Miyamura was frequently visiting the Flower Mansion, trying to persuade me to leave the church. The person attempting to deprogram Ms. Tomizawa was Pastor Mamoru Takazawa from the Christian Kobe True Church. Since Miyamura was close to Pastor Takazawa, he tried to assist him with the difficult task of persuading Ms. Tomizawa.

After a year and three months of captivity, Ms. Tomizawa managed to escape in September 1998. Shortly after her escape, she came to Tokyo for physical and mental care, where she met with Mr. Ohta, who was handling the abduction and confinement cases.

Ms. Tomizawa shared with Mr. Ohta a story that had weighed on her mind throughout her captivity—Miyamura had told her, "I've been in Tokyo trying to persuade him for two and a half years, but he still resists. His name is Goto."

Ms. Tomizawa then said, "It's been six months since I heard that. So, it's been three years since he was confined. If you haven't received a letter of renunciation from Mr. Goto, he's still being held."

Shocked by the revelation that a church member had been confined for three years, Mr. Ohta was struck by the name "Goto." When the security guard called to report that someone had been confined for nearly thirteen years and had just been freed, and mentioned the name "Goto," Mr. Ohta immediately recalled the story Ms. Tomizawa had shared with him.

Three years before Ms. Tomizawa's escape in 1998 was 1995. Now, in 2008, if he had been confined for thirteen years, it meant his confinement must have started in 1995. When the details from Ms. Tomizawa's testimony matched the security guard's report, Mr. Ohta reportedly shouted into the phone at the security guard:

"It's him. There's no mistake. He's not a suspicious person.

He's the real deal. Let him in and help him."

The fact that the security guard had contacted Mr. Ohta was as fortunate for me as the moment I met the female believer on the streets of Shoto.

I shared the story of my twelve years and five months of confinement with Mr. Ohta. As I spoke about the unbearable trials and repeated attacks on me, and how God had protected and helped me, I became so overwhelmed with emotion that I was left speechless and just wept. I had to pause my story each time the tears flowed.

Mr. Ohta listened attentively, carefully observing me. His main concern was my mental state. Having interviewed many victims of abduction and confinement, he was well aware of how deeply such experiences could leave scars on a person's psyche. He had seen firsthand how some victims displayed clear symptoms of post-traumatic stress disorder or PTSD, such as flinching at the sound of a knock on the door, collapsing in fear when reminded of their confinement, or even losing control of their bladder from terror.

After hearing my story, Mr. Ohta seemed to conclude that I hadn't experienced a mental breakdown.

Shortly after Mr. Ohta arrived at the church headquarters, Mr. Norishige Kondo, a person from the General Affairs Department who was well-versed in abduction and confinement issues, also came to the headquarters. Mr. Kondo explained that he had been imprisoned at the Ogikubo Glory Church in 1987, the same year I was first confined, and that he had met both my family and me. He particularly recalled having spoken with my brother often, although I only had vague memories of it.

At Mr. Ohta's and Mr. Kondo's request, I once again recounted the experiences of my twelve years and five months in detail. Having had no one to share it with all this time, I poured out everything I had kept bottled up inside to them.

When I looked at the clock on the wall, it was past 11:00 p.m. Mr. Ohta suggested, "It's time to rest." With nowhere else to go, I was given a place to stay in the adjacent tatami room. I couldn't stand up due to the intense pain in my knees, so Mr. Ohta and Mr. Kondo each supported me under my arms and helped me to the tatami room, where I finally lay down. However, I could hardly even go to the bathroom on my own. Seeing my difficulty in being alone at the church headquarters, both of them became concerned that I might have developed serious health issues after more than twelve years of confinement.

So, Mr. Kondo carried me on his back to a taxi, and we headed to Isshin Hospital in Toshima Ward for emergency care.

My Counterattack Begins

When I arrived at the hospital, a wheelchair was already prepared for me.

The doctor who saw me was a male internist. Upon seeing me with my clothes rolled up to my neck, he commented, "You've lost quite a bit of weight." He placed his stethoscope on my chest and back, and then asked, "What happened to your legs?" I briefly explained the situation.

He asked me to weigh myself, but since I couldn't stand up from the wheelchair, a nurse helped me onto the scale. Because I also wasn't able to stand unsupported, I quickly stepped off the scale when the nurse let go, and it read 39.2 kg. There's a back-story about this: I couldn't stand on the scale long enough for the number to stabilize, so the 39.2 kg reading was likely lower than it should have been. In the end, while my exact weight when I was released is uncertain, it was certainly under 50 kg. Even so, for someone who is 182 cm tall like me, that would result in a BMI below 16, which is considered dangerously underweight.

The doctor diagnosed me with severe malnutrition and stated that I was unable to walk and needed hospitalization, so I was immediately admitted. Further tests revealed malnutrition, anemia, generalized muscle weakness, and disuse muscle atrophy (a condition where muscles shrink and weaken due to lack of use).

At 1:40 a.m., I was moved from the examination room to Room 405 on the fourth floor of the hospital.

Room 405 was a large room with six beds. I was wheeled into the room, and since I had difficulty walking, a portable toilet was provided for me.

Although it was a time when I would usually be asleep, I couldn't fall asleep right away because I was so excited. The feeling of sleeping in such a completely different environment felt surreal. Just half a day ago, I had still been trapped in Room 804. Now, even though I had been thrown out, lying in a hospital bed felt like a miracle, and I could sense that God had guided me here. My body was in pain, but the overwhelming sense of relief and the feeling of being loved by God filled my heart with joy. I couldn't stop smiling even though I knew it was strange for a patient to be smiling while being urgently admitted.

I was so exhausted that I eventually fell asleep. When I woke up the next morning, I felt better than I had in a long time. A nurse greeted me with a smile and asked, "How do you feel?"

After taking my temperature, I had breakfast, and a completely new routine began.

In the afternoon, Mr. Ohta visited my hospital room.

"How are you feeling?" he asked.

"My legs are still the same, but I'm feeling good," I replied.

Mr. Ohta handed me a plastic bag with new underwear and an envelope.

"This is from the headquarters. It's to help you get by for now," he said.

When I opened the envelope, I found some cash inside. "I'm so sorry for all of this. Thank you so much," I replied.

"If you need anything, don't hesitate to ask. I'll come by again," he said kindly.

I was deeply grateful for his thoughtfulness.

It was 9:00 p.m. The lights in the large room were turned off, signaling bedtime.

During my confinement, I had been used to going to bed around 11:00 p.m., so I couldn't fall asleep right away. I lay in bed, lost in my thoughts.

Even on the morning of my release, I had continued my early

morning prayers, and the many blessings I had received from God were invaluable and precious. Because of this, much of the resentment I had felt toward my family had been cleansed. Although the fear embedded in my mind by my family still lingered, my feelings of hatred and bitterness had mostly calmed. More than anything, I was overwhelmed by God's love that even embraced those who had confined me, which I had felt during my prayers.

As the night passed and the date changed to February 12, around 1:00 a.m., a thought suddenly came to me. *If I can't sleep, then I'll pray.*

I positioned myself for prayer, leaning my back against the wall. Because of the pain, I couldn't sit cross-legged, so I stretched my legs out in front of me.

Having been given this newfound freedom, I decided to sincerely ask God what He wanted me to do next.

Not to disturb the other patients in the room, I prayed quietly: "Heavenly Father, what path should I take? What is Your will? Please show me."

Then, something felt different from my usual early morning prayers. It was as if a deep rumble, like an earthquake, was approaching. A powerful surge of emotion seemed to flood toward me. I stopped praying and focused my attention on God. It felt like a wave of anger. I had never experienced anything like this in my prayers before, and I was confused.

A voice echoed in my heart, like a storm:

Counterattack! Crush the enemy.

It was shocking. This was a furious God, unlike any I had

encountered in my previous prayers. Had my mind become distorted from the long confinement?

I questioned God.

"Heavenly Father, what should I do?"

File a lawsuit. Take them to court.

I was overwhelmed and confused.

People without experience in faith or prayer might dismiss my experience as nothing more than my own desires projecting onto my thoughts. Even those who follow another religion might think the same. Or they might assume that I am trying to manipulate God to suit my needs. Christians who view the Unification Church as a heresy might think, "That's the work of an evil spirit."

Even if that's what people think, this is the truth of what I experienced.

In the afternoon, Mr. Kondo came to visit me.

"Mr. Kondo, is there something wrong with me?"

I shared the shocking experience I had during my prayer earlier that morning and asked if perhaps my mind had been affected by the long confinement.

"It seems normal to me," Mr. Kondo replied. Then, he suggested, "Maybe it's truly a message from God. You should pray more about it."

That evening, when I prayed again, the result was the same.

During my prayer, a Bible verse came to mind: Be strong and courageous; don't be terrified or afraid of them. For it is the Lord your God who goes with you; He will not leave you or forsake you.

I took this as a message from God meant for me.

The following day, February 14, I made a vow in my prayer to follow God's will.

That day, I made the decision to pursue legal action.

The Reason I Cannot Forgive

"What we must do is love our enemies. We must not seek revenge or try to destroy them. Instead, by loving our enemies, we aim to liberate them."

I have always been particularly moved by this passage by Reverend Moon. In his collection of sermons, *God's Will and the World*, it is written: "Reverend Moon's philosophy is simple, and the principle is equally simple. By adopting the attitude of loving your enemies and putting it into practice, you can overcome anything. No obstacle will stand in your way."

In the New Testament, Jesus Christ commanded his disciples, "Love your enemies and pray for those who persecute you." Furthermore, while being crucified, he prayed for those who were trying to kill him, saying, "Father, forgive them," interceding on behalf of the Jewish people for their sins. The "love for enemies" that Reverend Moon teaches is exactly the same love that Jesus Christ exemplified.

Reverend Moon emphasized that we should not hate, seek revenge, or hold grudges even toward those who persecute us. Instead, we should love them. This is the same principle of "love your enemies" that has appeared throughout this book.

In the final days of World War II, Reverend Moon was accused of being a communist spy in Seoul, South Korea, and endured brutal torture by Japanese police in an attempt to force him to reveal the names of his associates. Despite this, Reverend Moon forgave his tormentors and even prayed for their well-being.

Then, at the end of World War II, the Japanese officers of the Gyeonggi Provincial Police who had tortured him found themselves isolated and in a dangerous situation. But it was Reverend Moon who reached out to help them safely return to Japan.

After the war, Reverend Moon focused on missionary work in what is now North Korea. However, he was wrongfully imprisoned and sent to a forced labor camp. Amidst harsh conditions and hunger, many prisoners died, but Reverend Moon endured for two years and eight months while still working relentlessly. After the 1950 Inchon invasion, the tide turned in the Korean War, and labor camp guards began killing prisoners before they could escape. Thanks to the Inchon attack, though, Reverend Moon was miraculously released just before his execution and thus narrowly escaped death.

With this background, Reverend Moon and North Korea Chairman Kim Il-sung could truly be described as the "enemy of enemies," but Reverend Moon dedicated his heart and soul for the sake of Kim Il-sung and North Korea.

Throughout his life, Reverend Moon was wrongfully imprisoned multiple times and faced life-threatening situations. If I had to sum up his life in one word, it would be "miraculous." Why do miracles happen? According to Reverend Moon, it's because the living God protected, guided, and helped him. Furthermore, regardless of the unjust treatment he endured, Reverend Moon lived according to God's will and loved his enemies.

I consciously chose to follow the noble philosophy of Reverend Moon's life.

Even in the face of unreasonable treatment, I made a firm resolution never to hate, hold a grudge, or resort to violence. Just as God protected and helped Reverend Moon loving his enemies, I believed that loving my enemies was God's will for me, and that God would be the fortress protecting both my heart and my body.

However, this was no easy task.

Confined to an apartment, I was relentlessly attacked by those who sought to destroy the very object of my faith, something I held more dearly than my own life. When I protested the injustice of abduction and confinement, I was met with mocking laughter and insults. When I tried to escape, the scene turned into a battle-field—blood was spilled, and my body became covered in bruises.

Continually exposed to such a surreal environment, my heart was overwhelmed by feelings of anger and resentment so intense that—along with a deep loneliness, fear, and despair—it made me wish for death. Above all, I had to relentlessly battle the waves of hatred toward those who had taken away my freedom.

Sadly, I came to realize that noble love, such as "loving your enemies," was completely absent in me. Instead of loving them, I was struggling just to rid myself of feelings of resentment. Even the slightest lapse in vigilance would cause dark, venomous hatred to rise within me, like a coiled serpent. Each time this happened, I would repeat Reverend Moon's words like a mantra, reflecting on his life's journey, and then pray, clinging to God.

I believe the reason my heart didn't completely break under the extreme conditions of confinement was because of my prayers to God and my efforts to remove resentment and hatred from my heart by meditating on Reverend Moon's teachings.

At the same time, I recognize that forced deprogramming through abduction and confinement is an absolute violation of human rights and a criminal act.

The place of confinement becomes a lawless zone, a sealed-off space where violence can easily occur. Faith, which is more precious than life itself, is forcibly stripped away in these isolated environments. The fear and suffering of being forced to abandon one's faith in a space with no escape is beyond words. For example, there was a twenty-seven-year-old woman who was driven to suicide. A twenty-five-year-old man, attempting to escape, fell from the sixth-floor balcony of the confinement location and suffered life-threatening injuries, eventually resulting in memory loss. A woman was raped by a deprogramming specialist. Many victims continue to bear the psychological scars of their confinement, and many develop PTSD.

Since Pastor Satoshi Moriyama, founder of Ogikubo Glory Church, started deprogramming in 1966 under the belief that the Unification Church was a "heresy," over 4,300 members have fallen victim to abduction and forced deprogramming. Such things have happened in a nation that prides itself on its freedom, democracy, and rule of law. At the very least, the God I prayed to and believed in was filled with anger. He commanded that evil should never be pardoned, and that we must battle against it.

Me (front row, center) before being abducted and confined.
Taken around spring 1995 at "Hishokan" in Tokyo.

The Flower Mansion building, where I was confined.
The confinement took place in a corner room on
the eighth and top floor.

The Flower Mansion building

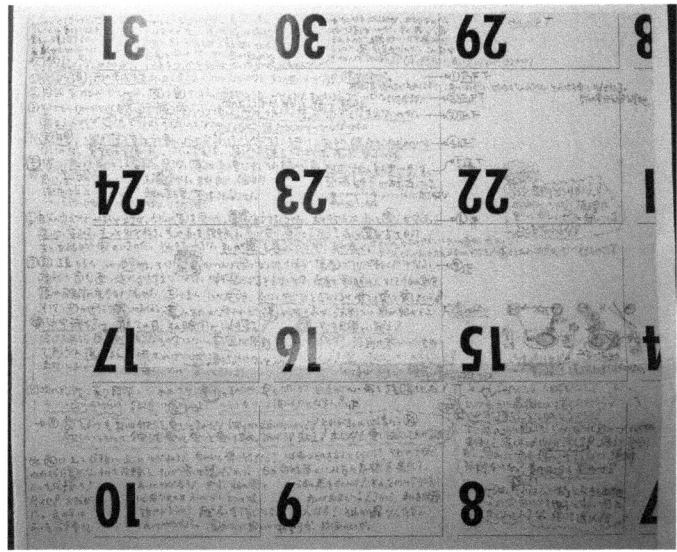

A scrap of calendar paper on which messages from God were written during the 11th year of confinement, around 2007.

Me (left) participating in a street rally with fellow believers after being freed from confinement. Taken in August 2008 in front of JR Ogikubo Station.

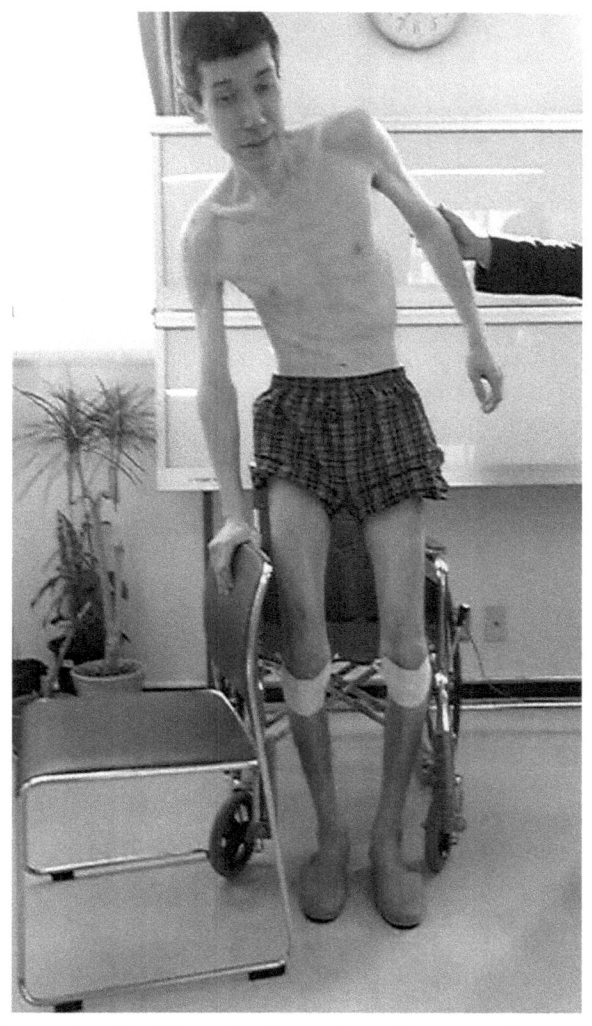

Me on the third day after being freed from confinement.
Journalist Kazuhiro Yonemoto took this photo on
February 13, 2008. At the hospital, I was diagnosed with
malnutrition, generalized muscle weakness, disuse muscle
atrophy, and anemia

In front of the Tokyo District Court following the first trial verdict. January 28, 2014.

Press conference at the Judicial Press Club following
the appellate court ruling on November 13, 2014.
Left: Lawyer Nobuya Fukumoto, the representative.
Right: Mamoru Kamono, the Director of Public Relations
(at that time).

Chapter 4

The Fight To Get It Back

New Start and Criminal Accusation

"Captain Goto survived his confinement."

Fellow believers who had once walked alongside me came to my hospital room, one after another. News spread quickly that I had been freed after twelve years and five months of confinement. It was said that the force of it was beyond words, a storm of astonishment and joy.

My fellow believers had changed in appearance with age, but familiar, nostalgic faces appeared by my bedside every day. While everyone was filled with joy that they couldn't hide, they were bewildered by my drastically altered appearance. When I started to share my experiences of what had happened since I disappeared from their lives, many of them were moved to tears. The heartfelt emotions, warm words, and flowing tears from these fellow believers deeply touched my heart, which had long been exposed to cold, distant relationships.

Among the many visitors who came to see me, there was one person who wasn't a member of the Unification Church. He came with Mr. Kondo from the General Affairs office three days after my release from confinement.

Mr. Kondo came to me and said, "There's someone who would like to visit you, Goto-san. Would you like to meet him?"

"Who is it?" I asked.

"He is a reportage writer covering the issue of abduction and confinement."

When I heard the words "reportage writer," I was taken aback. Given that the Unification Church had been heavily criticized by the media, I assumed that any reporter interested in the church would have a critical viewpoint.

"Is it alright to meet him?" I asked.

"Well, you'll see once you meet him. He wants to talk to you, so I've booked a meeting room," Mr. Kondo said with a playful grin.

I transferred from my bed to a wheelchair, and Mr. Kondo wheeled me to the meeting room on the fifth floor of the hospital.

The meeting room was spacious, about the size of twenty tatami mats, with a long table and several chairs.

"Are you Mr. Goto? I'm Kazuhiro Yonemoto," said a small, elderly man, giving me a box wrapped in paper with a friendly smile. "I'm not sure if this will suit your taste, but I brought this for you."

At first glance, it was clear that it was a box of chocolates. During my confinement, I was never allowed to eat chocolate, and it was something I had longed for desperately. The nurses had advised me to avoid eating sweets suddenly, but just the thought of devouring the entire box filled me with excitement.

Mr. Yonemoto, sitting across from me at the long table, expressed concern for my condition. Then he said, "I heard you were confined for twelve years. That must have been incredibly difficult. Would you be willing to share your story?"

After listening to me, Mr. Yonemoto said, "I'm sorry, but would you mind taking off your clothes?"

I was taken aback by the request, but since there was no one else in the meeting room except the three of us, I took off my top, leaving only my undershirt.

"Could you take off your shirt, too?" he asked.

I hesitated for a moment but did as he asked. Mr. Yonemoto's eyes were fixed on my body.

"Is it okay if I take some pictures?" he asked, turning to Mr. Kondo. "Kondo-san, your phone has a camera, right? Could I borrow it?"

When Mr. Kondo handed over his phone, Mr. Yonemoto pointed the lens at me. "Could you stretch your arms out like this?" He demonstrated the pose and then took several pictures.

"Could you take off your pants, too?"

"The pants, too?"

I hesitated for a moment but removed my sweatpants, leaving only my underwear. At that, Mr. Yonemoto seemed surprised and let out a sound.

"This is terrible," he said.

He seemed shocked by how thin my legs had become—they were like sticks. Then, as if he were a photographer directing a model, Mr. Yonemoto quickly started giving instructions. "Could

155

you place your feet on this chair?" "Could you raise your hands?"

He kept changing angles and snapping pictures.

"If possible, could you stand up?"

Unable to stand on my own, I relied on Mr. Kondo for support and managed to get up, but the pain in my knees was so intense that I couldn't hold the pose for more than a few seconds. Mr. Yonemoto carefully timed it and captured my best attempt at standing with his phone camera.

The photos Mr. Yonemoto took in his effort to document the situation would later become crucial evidence in the legal battle. However, at that moment, I didn't fully grasp the significance of having those photos taken.

Later, I found out that Mr. Yonemoto was a reportage writer who specialized in new religions and had a high reputation in the field. While much of his work had a critical focus, he had become interested in the issue of captivity of Unification Church members. He was gathering information for a book on confinement and forced deprogramming; that book, *Our Unpleasant Neighbor*, was published in July 2008.

He had been writing the book in February 2008 when he heard that a Unification Church member had been released after a long-term confinement and was urgently hospitalized. He immediately rushed to the hospital to interview me and include me in his book.

Since I had received a clear message from God, which changed my perspective about how to respond to my kidnapping and confinement, I told Mr. Kondo I wanted to pursue legal action.

"I'm thinking of suing those people. What should I do?" I said.

"When you say suing, do you mean criminal charges?" he asked.

"Yes."

"That's a big decision," he said.

"There was a strong push from God to do so," I replied.

Mr. Kondo then explained the process, from criminal charges to trial and verdict. The conversation naturally shifted to who would be the targets of the lawsuit. The individuals I planned to sue were Miyamura, Pastor Matsunaga, my mother, my older brother, his wife, and my sister. As we discussed these people, I mentioned how much my mother had loved me since I was young. Mr. Kondo quietly said: "Goto-san, do you think you can handle this?"

"What do you mean?" I asked.

"If the criminal process moves forward and an indictment is made, your mother will have to sit in the defendant's seat. Can you testify properly in front of her?"

I couldn't answer right away.

"It's not just that. If there's a guilty verdict, your mother and other family members could end up in prison as criminals."

This is what it means to file criminal charges against your parents and siblings, he added.

Confronted with the reality of how the criminal trial would unfold, I was surprisingly shaken by my own emotions. The thought of my mother and my family standing in the defendant's seat was enough to tighten my chest. The reason many victims of confinement never took their cases to court was likely because of the deep resistance they felt toward suing their own parents and siblings.

I realized that I was crossing my arms and had let out a heavy sigh. I needed to rethink the significance of filing criminal charges once again.

My family, out of love and concern for me, no doubt believed they were doing the right thing by abducting and confining me. However, the decision to abduct and confine me wasn't something they came up with on their own—it was based on the advice of Pastor Matsunaga and Miyamura, whom they had consulted, and they were influenced by their guidance. My family must have thought, based on the thousands of successful cases in the past, that abducting and confining me wouldn't be considered a crime if it was done to get a Unification Church member to renounce his faith.

However, trying to force someone to leave their faith through abduction and confinement, even if it's done by parents or siblings, is a violation of religious freedom. It's a crime involving *Capture and Confinement* and *Compulsion* that clearly breaks the law. I needed to make sure my family understood that locking me in a room and forcing me to abandon my faith was a criminal act. If this issue remained unclear, there would be no chance of rebuilding my relationship with them.

Also, this wasn't just about me and my family. While I had been locked up, many other Unification Church members had fallen victim to abduction and confinement. The bubble economy period was marked by widespread abductions and confinements, and these crimes continued even afterward. If I didn't speak out, wouldn't the suffering of the victims persist unchecked? Above all, God was urging me to fight this battle.

I told Mr. Kondo firmly, "It's alright. I won't back down."

With that, I began working on a statement for the criminal charges.

About ten days after my hospitalization, the hospital, suspecting the criminal nature of my case based on my physical condition and testimony, contacted the nearby Sugamo Police Station, which led to rapid developments.

To file the criminal charges, I was introduced to a lawyer by the Unification Church headquarters. The lawyer, Nobuya Fukumoto, was a former prosecutor at the Tokyo District Public Prosecutors Office and had extensive experience with criminal cases.

In late March, once I was able to walk on my own, I visited his office in Kōjimachi, Chiyoda Ward, for a meeting. My first impression of Lawyer Fukumoto was that he had the sharp, focused demeanor that reflected his days as a prosecutor.

When I briefly recounted the events of my abduction and confinement, as I always did, Lawyer Fukumoto was astonished.

"You managed to endure for twelve years. I truly admire your mental strength," he said.

That day, Lawyer Fukumoto instructed me to write down the facts in as much detail as possible, in chronological order, so I finally began preparing for the criminal charges.

Meanwhile, my health improved significantly.

About two weeks after my hospitalization, the pain in my knees began to ease, and by March, I was able to walk with crutches on my own. Although the hospital food was simple, when compared to the meager meals I had during my confinement, the portions were much larger and had a variety of side dishes. As a result, my weight gradually increased, and the legs that had become painfully thin—diagnosed as disuse muscle atrophy—started to gain some muscle through rehabilitation.

On March 31, I was discharged from hospital. After fifty days in the hospital, my weight had returned to 65 kgs. While my body hadn't fully recovered, I was slowly able to climb and descend stairs.

However, when it came time to return to social life, both I and my surroundings had changed significantly since my confinement. I stumbled right from the moment I left the hospital.

I first had to look for a place to live. But because my social credibility had been damaged, renting an apartment was quite difficult.

Eventually, through the help of an acquaintance, I was able to rent an apartment in Tokyo. But then came the next challenge—finding a job. When I tried to write my resume, I realized there was a blank of twelve years and five months that I couldn't explain. Also, my driver's license had expired, and I was left wondering if I would have to start over to get my license again. That's when I met a business owner who said, "Your mental strength in enduring confinement is impressive. I'd like you to work for my company." I was fortunate to find someone who valued what I had lost.

Still, the challenges didn't end there.

Perhaps due to the effects of my confinement, my eyesight, which had been 1.5 before the abduction, had dropped to 0.2, and it was becoming difficult to function without glasses. So, when I decided to buy glasses and took the JR Yamanote Line for the first time in a while, I noticed that all the passengers around me were intently staring at something in their hands. They were moving their fingers quickly to type messages on their cell phones.

Although mobile phones existed in 1995 when I was confined, only a few people out of a hundred were likely to use them, and there were no users around me. However, twelve years later, when I was released from confinement, almost everyone was using a mobile phone. For someone like me, who hadn't experienced this major cultural shift, seeing so many people in the same posture, typing messages on their phones, seemed strange.

I was also surprised when I passed through the station ticket gate. The person in front of me held something up to the top of the gate and walked straight through. It was an IC card, *Suica*, which was part of an automated fare system. I was amazed at the progress of technology and how convenient things had become.

The spread of personal computers was another surprise. In 1995, computers were only used by professionals in specialized departments or accounting offices. Microsoft's Windows 95 had been released two months after I was abducted, and I had no idea it had become such a hit. However, after my release from confinement, when I spoke with some of my fellow believers, I learned that many of them used personal computers with ease as if it were completely normal.

As I began rebuilding my life and reintegrating into society, I realized just how disconnected I had been from the world between the ages of thirty-one and forty-four. I was constantly shocked by all the changes. I felt like I was a modern-day *Urashima Taro.** I tried to control my anxiety by facing each challenge one by one and working through them.

In early April, shortly after my discharge, the Sugamo Police Station contacted the hospital, informing them that they had decided to transfer my case to the Ogikubo Police Station. They also wanted to conduct a brief interview with me before the transfer.

On April 8, I was questioned by the criminal division at the Sugamo Police Station in the hospital's meeting room. It was my first time being questioned, and I felt nervous, but the kind-looking officer started the conversation casually.

"Urashima Taro" is a Japanese children's tale about a young fisherman who rescues a small sea turtle. It turns out that the little turtle was the daughter of the Emperor of Sea. Another turtle comes to give the fisherman gills and take him under the sea to the Dragon Palace (Ryugujo), where the princess Otohime entertains him as a reward for saving her life. The fisherman spends a few days with the princess but then becomes lonely for his aged mother and asks to return home. Otohime gives him a jeweled box (tamatebako) that will protect him but warns him not to open it. Once home, the young fisherman is shocked to learn he has been gone for several hundred years and everything in his life has vanished. One day, he opens the box and immediately starts to grow old. Before he dies, he hears the princess' voice saying, "I told you not too open that box. In it was your old age."

It seems like you've been through a terrible experience. I truly feel sorry for you," he said.

The officer explained that since the Flower Mansion, where I was last confined, was under the jurisdiction of the Ogikubo Police Station, my case would need to be transferred to them.

He also commented, "I don't know how the Ogikubo Police Station will handle this case, but I want you to understand that cases involving family members are generally quite difficult."

"Difficult, in what way? Are you saying the charges will be difficult?" I asked.

"This is just a general observation," he replied.

Was he implying that there would be no intervention in civil matters? However, what my family had done clearly fell under Criminal Law Article 221, *Unlawful Capture or Confinement Causing Death or Injury.*

I had things I wanted to say, but since it had already been decided that the case would be transferred from Sugamo Police Station, I thought it would be inappropriate to make any demands. I decided to simply listen to the officer, and the interview ended.

By late April, the case had been handed from Sugamo Police Station to the Ogikubo Police Station.

In June, I filed a complaint with the Ogikubo Police Station, accusing six individuals of "Unlawful Capture or Confinement Causing Death or Injury" and "Attempted Compulsion." The accused were company president Takashi Miyamura, Pastor Yasutomo Matsunaga of the Niitsu Evangelical Church, as well as my mother, brother, sister-in-law, and sister.

As evidence, I submitted my detailed statement, a doctor's diagnosis, and photographs of my emaciated condition taken by Mr. Yonemoto three days after my release from confinement.

After a while, the Ogikubo Police Station contacted Lawyer Fukumoto.

"Since the victim's family is involved in this case, it needs to be handled with care. First, we will interview Mr. Goto's mother. After that, we will update you on the results."

The Ogikubo Police Station made a copy of the complaint and returned the original to me. They informed me that they would temporarily withhold acceptance of the complaint for further review, but the investigation would begin at the end of June.

In August, the Ogikubo Police Station officially accepted the complaint, and I was summoned to the station for what would be the first round of questioning.

The station is located about a ten-minute bus ride from JR Ogikubo Station, along Ome Kaido, roughly two kilometers west of the Flower Mansion, where I had been confined. After I checked in, I was escorted to the criminal division, passing by several officers working at their desks, and then led into a small room, about the size of a three-tatami-mat space. The room was bare, with only a computer and printer on the desk, resembling the interrogation rooms seen in crime dramas. I sat down the chair, and the questioning began immediately.

The officer in charge was a middle-aged man with fair skin and a solid build. Perhaps to ease my nerves, he spoke to me in a friendly manner.

As I answered his questions, the officer typed my responses into the computer. Once the document was ready, he printed it out and read it aloud. If there were no errors, I was asked to sign and seal the document, which would then be my official statement.

The official statement would become an important piece of evidence. I had to recount the details of the confinement as accurately as possible, but since no lawyer or companion was allowed to be with me during the questioning, I felt extremely nervous.

I carefully chose my words while trying to recall my memories, but providing the precise wording to the officer's questions was challenging. I did not have exact memories of every event that took place for more than a decade, especially during the months when I was severely depressed or starving. Thus, some details had become fuzzy, and there were things I could only partially remember.

I completed and signed the statement, but on the bus ride back from the Ogikubo Police Station, I found myself regretting some of my comments—"Maybe I should have phrased that part differently." But once the statement was signed, it couldn't be corrected.

I visited the Ogikubo Police Station about ten times for questioning and the preparation of my statement, with each session lasting about ninety minutes to two hours. In addition to that, I had to identify the apartment where I had been confined for about six months before being moved to the Flower Mansion. Since I was moved at night, I didn't know the building's name or even its location.

Guided by the officer, we went to a building near JR Ogikubo Station.

"Is this the building?" the officer asked.

"I don't think so. There's no pipe-like structure on the wall," I replied.

During my confinement, I had seen part of the wall through the window. The outer wall on the balcony side had a unique design, with iron pipes running vertically along it.

"Let's try this one," the officer said.

We walked for about a minute, and the officer pointed to a building. "How about this one?"

"This is it."

The outer wall, which I had only seen partially from the inside, was now fully visible. The apartment was on the sixth floor, Room 605.

With that, the process of confirming the apartment was complete.

Even though the family had been questioned and the building identified, I suspected the officer might have taken me to an unrelated building to test the accuracy of my memory.

As I went through the questioning, I became increasingly anxious about having no papers or other tangible proof of what happened to me.

For a criminal case to move forward, objective evidence is important.

In the closet of Room 804, I had written a diary that detailed the conditions of my confinement. That diary described in detail the situation when I tried to escape and was subdued by force. However, since I had been thrown out with only my clothes, I couldn't grab the diary or any other physical evidence.

I knew my family would destroy my records or documents from their interactions with Miyamura or Pastor Matsunaga, as these would have been evidence of the confinement. I wanted the police to quickly arrest them, so their homes could be searched for evidence of the crimes. But I saw no signs of arrests or searches.

While I was undergoing intense questioning and statement preparation, it seemed the police were also questioning my family and the accused. However, the police were only doing voluntary interviews with the accused. I feared that, if this continued, they would cover up the evidence and collude to bury the truth.

During these difficult times, what kept me going was the support from my fellow believers.

The movement to end abduction and confinement began to gain momentum as more people became outraged after learning about my case. In July 2008, my fellow believers gathered near the north exit of JR Ogikubo Station, launching street campaigns to raise awareness about the reality of abduction and confinement at the scene of the incident. They held banners, handed out leaflets with details of the case, and used loudspeakers to speak to passersby.

By October, a citizens' group called the *Association to End Abduction and Confinement* was formed with the aim of eradicating deprogramming through abduction and confinement. The street campaigns at Ogikubo Station continued for more than two years.

An Unfair Decision

What had become of her?

Throughout my confinement and even after my release, I was constantly worried about my fiancée, Ms. B.

When I asked the church headquarters to find out about her, I learned that she had already married another man and had children. I also learned that for three and a half years, she had believed my promise, "I will definitely come back. Please believe in me," and waited for my return. However, when she turned thirty-four years old, she faced an unavoidable decision. She was reaching an age where pregnancy and childbirth were becoming risky, and those around her began expressing concerns about the risks of having a child later in life. In the end, she gave up on marrying me.

I heard through someone that Ms. B was very happy about my release from confinement, saying, "I'm so glad. This is such a big deal." I felt a sense of relief, not only to learn how well she was doing but also to hear her kind words.

Then, in the fall of 2008, I met someone new. I took part in a Blessing Ceremony with the woman I was introduced to, and by the end of the year, we were married and living together. Finally, in my mid-forties, I was able to start a family of my own.

On February 2, 2009, just as my new life was beginning, the Ogikubo Police Station sent my case to the Tokyo District Public Prosecutors Office.

On February 9, I visited the Tokyo office for the first time and met the officer from the Ogikubo Police Station who had been in charge of my questioning. The Tokyo office is located in the government district of Kasumigaseki, Chiyoda Ward. After getting off at Kasumigaseki Station on the Marunouchi subway line, I walked a short distance and saw the massive government building. It was much larger than I expected.

The Ogikubo officer was waiting for me in front of the main gate.

"It's been a while. How have you been?" he asked.

I returned the greeting and looked up at the imposing government building that towered over me.

"This is the Tokyo District Public Prosecutors Office, right?"

"Yes. Let's go."

After registering, I confirmed the floor and room number where the questioning would take place with the officer.

"Well then, I'll leave you here."

"Thank you for everything," I said. This was where I parted ways with the officer.

When I entered the room, there were two men inside. The older of the two stood up and said,

"Mr. Toru Goto, correct?"

"Yes."

"Please come this way."

The man who spoke was the prosecutor.

"I believe you're familiar with the process since you've already been questioned by the police, but we also need to prepare an official statement here. Some of the questions may overlap with what you've already been asked, so please understand," the prosecutor said.

He maintained a dignified and detached demeanor, proceeding with the questioning in a calm way. The other man typed everything into the computer.

The Tokyo District Public Prosecutors Office's questioning sessions with me continued for almost two months, until March 31.

The conviction rate in Japan's criminal trials is 99.9%. Once you're indicted, a guilty verdict is almost certain. I kept reflecting on this fact.

A year and a half after my release from confinement, in August 2009, a national movement to end abduction and confinement was launched, with advocacy events held at Unification Church branches all over Japan. This movement continued through October, and I traveled across Japan, from Hokkaido in the north to Miyazaki in the south, sharing my experience as a victim of abduction and confinement and calling for cooperation to resolve the issue.

We explained that since 1966, there had been an alarming number of cases—4,300—of confinement and deprogramming. While various efforts had been made to prevent these crimes, and the number of cases had decreased from the peak of 375 in 1992, abduction and confinement had still not been eradicated. Among

Unification Church members, even if someone had never personally experienced abduction and confinement, most had friends or fellow members who had been victims and felt the pain of those experiences. Everywhere I went, people who were newly exposed to the horrors of abduction and confinement reacted with intense anger, and the events were always charged with emotion.

The movement also spread internationally. In September, I traveled to the United States. In cities like New York and Chicago, I met with Christian pastors and human rights activists to raise awareness about the realities of abduction and confinement. In August 2009, advocacy meetings were held in Seoul, South Korea, and in December, I visited twelve cities in Korea to share my experience.

In December that year, I received some encouraging news, which helped ease my concerns about the lack of physical evidence. A female believer came forward and said she had witnessed my confinement in the Flower Mansion.

This woman had been confined by her family on the fifth floor of the Flower Mansion and forced to renounce. As a former believer, she came to visit me in Room 804 along with Miyamura and other former believers. So, she was able to testify about how I had been confined and forced to deprogram. Later, after going through many struggles, she returned to the Unification Church, and when she heard that I had been released, she was shocked, saying, "I can't believe you were confined there for ten years after that." I clearly remembered her as well.

Having an eyewitness to my confinement was important, and

I had her write a statement and began preparing to submit it as additional evidence to the Tokyo District Public Prosecutors Office.

However, a few days later, on December 9, 2009, the Tokyo District Public Prosecutors Office informed me they had decided not to prosecute, citing "Insufficient Suspicion." At the time, I was traveling in Korea, and when I heard the news, I was stunned and disoriented.

"Insufficient Suspicion." This was different from "Lack of Suspicion," where the accused is considered not guilty, or "Suspension of Prosecution," where there's no need for a trial. "Insufficient Suspicion" meant that although the suspicion of a crime hadn't been completely cleared, there was no conclusive evidence that could lead to a conviction in court.

The Prosecutors Office said they couldn't bring the case to trial due to a lack of solid evidence. But neither the Ogikubo police nor the prosecutor arrested any of the accused, nor did they carry out any forced searches or investigations. Only voluntary questioning was conducted. During this time, the accused had plenty of opportunities to erase their evidence or collude to cover up their actions. It was extremely difficult to obtain confessions or any evidence from them.

I had always believed my case was so extreme that it would be easily prosecuted, but the way the police and prosecutor were handling it left me with an uneasy feeling. If my case could be dismissed due to "insufficient" evidence, what would happen to other cases? Would the number of abduction and confinement cases involving Unification Church members continue to rise? I was filled with anger, and a cold chill ran down my spine.

Lawyer Fukumoto was also enraged.

"To not carry out a proper investigation and then claim there's not enough evidence to prosecute—it's clear that the responsibility falls on the investigative authorities. It seems they intentionally shut down the case from the start with a predetermined conclusion. They have no sense of justice—what a pitiful group," he said.

Despite the decision not to prosecute, the movement to end abduction and confinement continued to gain momentum. On January 8, 2010, a volunteer organization called *Japan Victims' Association Against Religious Kidnapping and Forced Conversion* was founded, with me as the representative.

Two months after the decision not to prosecute, on February 12, 2010, I went to the Tokyo District Public Prosecutors Office with Lawyer Fukumoto. The purpose was to ask the prosecutor in charge why the case had been dismissed. This was also part of the preparation for filing a complaint with the Committee for the Inquest of Prosecution.

The Committee for the Inquest of Prosecution consists of a panel of eleven randomly selected citizens who review whether the decision to dismiss a case was appropriate. The system was created to ensure that public opinion is reflected in prosecutorial decisions and to promote the proper functioning of the criminal justice system.

The prosecutor who was first assigned to my case had been reassigned in April 2009. The new prosecutor told us that the case had been dismissed because the accused had consistently denied the abduction and confinement, and there was no evidence to bring the case to trial.

For example, my family admitted to locking the apartment's front door with a padlock, but they claimed it was only a temporary measure. They also said they feared members of the Unification Church might try to break in to rescue me and even use a chain cutter to cut the door chain from the outside.

I was absolutely stunned by their explanation that the padlock on the inside of the door was meant to prevent an attack from outside. Could the prosecutor really believe such a ridiculous and desperate lie?

"The padlock wasn't for preventing an external intrusion," Lawyer Fukumoto immediately retorted. "It was clearly used to stop the person inside from leaving. The purpose is obvious. It's nothing but confinement!"

Without hesitation, the prosecutor came up with an even more outrageous claim.

"Your family said they would have let you out if you had asked," he said calmly, without changing his expression. But Lawyer Fukumoto immediately fired back.

"That's ridiculous! Did the prosecutor honestly believe such an obvious lie? Twelve years—twelve years! Do you really expect me to believe that someone would stay there by choice and become so painfully thin? It's completely unreasonable!"

"It's difficult to completely dismiss the explanation provided by the family," the prosecutor said.

He then added, "Are you here to protest? Discussing it here won't change the decision."

Lawyer Fukumoto and I left the Tokyo District Public Prosecutors Office, both feeling frustrated and helpless.

"He has no intention of doing his job seriously. He's the worst kind of prosecutor. If people like him are running things, the future of the Prosecutors Office is in serious trouble," Lawyer Fukumoto said, his words filled with disgust. Perhaps his anger was even greater because he had once worked in the Tokyo District Public Prosecutors Office.

It was not easy to overturn a decision by filing a complaint with the Committee for the Inquest of Prosecution. Looking at past cases, it seemed nearly impossible. But I decided that as long as there was even a small chance, I would do everything I could.

To challenge the non-prosecution, I needed to present new evidence. I prepared the statement from the female believer who had witnessed the confinement, which had missed the deadline for submission last time, along with other supporting documents. On June 23, 2010, I submitted a complaint to the Committee for the Inquest of Prosecution.

The result from the commission, announced on October 6, 2010, was that *"non-prosecution deemed appropriate."*

"This is absolutely unacceptable. These people are out of their minds," Lawyer Fukumoto said when he called me on my mobile phone.

Unlike the secrecy of the Prosecutors Office, the results of the Committee for the Inquest of Prosecution's deliberations were made public, and the decision was sent to the applicant's lawyer as a "resolution notice." The notice that Lawyer Fukumoto shared with me was eleven pages long, printed on A4 paper.

After reading it, I was stunned. The content was so shocking and disheartening. Every claim I made had been rejected, and only the statements from the accused were acknowledged.

The resolution concluded with the following: *"To consider this case as Compulsion and Unlawful Capture or Confinement Causing Death or Injury raises many questions, and therefore, we have reached the conclusion as outlined in the resolution."*

Since only one complaint can be filed with the Committee for the Inquest of Prosecution, the path to criminal litigation was now closed.

The decision not to prosecute left me feeling defeated for a time. I never imagined the truth could be so distorted. Was it really impossible for the illegal acts of confinement and deprogramming against Unification Church members to be properly judged by the Japanese justice system?

I felt overwhelmed with sorrow for the fellow believers who had fought alongside me and supported the cause of ending abduction and confinement. Many Unification Church members still lived in fear of being abducted and confined. If I gave up now, what would happen? It would mean that even after more than twelve years of confinement, there would be no consequences for the kidnappers and deprogrammers, and we would be living in a lawless country where abductions could happen everywhere. This must be stopped at all costs.

The only way to address abduction and confinement in court now was with a civil lawsuit.

However, after being devastated by the disappointing outcome of the criminal case, I couldn't immediately bring myself to file a civil lawsuit. The unreasonable wording in the Committee for the Inquest of Prosecution's "resolution notice" weighed heavily on my heart, leaving me traumatized.

Filing a civil lawsuit would require a tremendous amount of time and effort once again, and even then, there was no guarantee of success. So, I threw myself into studying the issue. Gradually, hope began to emerge.

I realized that there had been many cases in the past where, even after criminal charges were dismissed, plaintiffs had won civil lawsuits for damages. Criminal trials, where the state punishes an individual, require a higher standard of proof than civil cases. This is why the principle of *innocent until proven guilty* exists.

In other words, the same evidence might be treated differently in criminal and civil cases.

To prevent the accused from destroying evidence or colluding, it is crucial to act fast in criminal charges. Speed was essential in preparing documents, such as written evidence. On the other hand, in civil lawsuit, there is more time to carefully prepare evidence and gather supporting materials.

To win a civil lawsuit, it's crucial to present strong arguments and solid evidence that will convince the judge.

I asked Lawyer Fukumoto if I had a chance of winning the civil lawsuit.

"We won't know unless we try," he said. Noticing my despondency, he added, "Well, we still have some time. Why don't you take a moment to think it over—maybe enjoy the autumn breeze?"

The prescription for filing a damages claim under civil law is three years. From the time I was released from confinement, I had until February 11, 2011, to file the lawsuit, meaning I only had four months left. I couldn't afford to delay my decision.

I also thought about this: In a civil lawsuit, both the plaintiff's and defendant's claims and evidence would be publicly examined in court, exposed to third parties. Through this process, I could raise awareness about the reality of abduction and confinement.

I took a moment to reflect on my twelve years and five months of unjust imprisonment.

Even if the defendants tried to cover up the facts and fabricate lies to counter my story, as long as the abduction and confinement were real, their claims would eventually fall apart. The truth is undeniable, and I held it in my hands. This was my greatest strength in pursuing the civil lawsuit.

On January 31, 2011, I filed the civil lawsuit at the Tokyo District Court.

One Against Six

The defendants in the civil lawsuit were Takashi Miyamura, Pastor Yasutomo Matsunaga, my brother, my sister-in-law, my sister, and Pastor Matsunaga's Japan Alliance Christ Church since the church held employer responsibility for him. This meant there was a single plaintiff against five defendants and one organization. The total amount of damages being claimed, including lost income and emotional distress, was 216,185,527 yen.

My mother, whose dementia had worsened, was excluded from the lawsuit. In November 2009, when I had filed the criminal charges, I received a registered letter from my sister informing me of her marriage and expressing deep disappointment that I had filed the criminal charges. The letter also mentioned my mother's dementia.

As in the criminal case, my legal representative was Lawyer Nobuya Fukumoto.

On the defendants' side, Takashi Miyamura was represented by Lawyers Hiroshi Yamaguchi and Sou Kimura.

Pastor Yasutomo Matsunaga was represented by Lawyers Shuji Nakamura and Reiko Higashi.

The three members of my family—my brother, sister-in-law,

and sister—were represented by Lawyers Takashi Yamaguchi and Morio Ogiue.

The Japan Alliance Christ Church was represented by Lawyer Eiichi Aoki.

Except for Lawyer Eiichi Aoki, who was a Christian and served as a trustee for the Japan Alliance Christ Church, the lawyers representing the defendants were from the National Network of Lawyers Against Spiritual Sales (Zenkoku Benren), led by Lawyer Hiroshi Yamaguchi. This group, also known as NNLASS, had long been opposed to the Unification Church. Given the lineup of defense lawyers, it was clear that this case was being taken extremely seriously. For those lawyers critical of the Unification Church, this lawsuit was undoubtedly one they could not afford to lose.

On March 22, 2011, the first oral arguments were held at the Tokyo District Court. The Great East Japan Earthquake had struck on March 11, and this disaster seemed to add to the heavy atmosphere that hung in the air in the courtroom.

The Tokyo District Court is located just behind the Tokyo District Public Prosecutors Office, where I had previously been questioned. As I made my way toward Courtroom 709, I noticed a crowd gathering in the hallway outside. After the oral arguments, I learned that 200 people had lined up for the forty-two available seats in the public gallery.

In the courtroom, Lawyer Fukumoto sat with me on the plaintiff's side, which was to the left when facing from the gallery. On the right, the defendants and their representatives entered one by one and took their seats.

The plaintiff's side and the defendant's side faced each other. I sat in the plaintiff's seat, and across from me, with the witness stand between us, sat my brother, sister-in-law, and sister in the defendant's seats. It had been three years since I was released from the Flower Mansion, and this was our first reunion. I stared at them intently, but they didn't meet my gaze. Miyamura was also seated on the defendant's side. The memories of my confinement came rushing back, along with a deep, inexpressible sense of darkness.

There were ten people in total sitting in the defendant's seats, as two defendants were absent for unknown reasons.

Facing the defendants, I could clearly sense the challenge of the trial. Even without the religious organization, I had to address the claims coming from three directions: Miyamura, Pastor Matsunaga, and my family. As the plaintiff, I knew I would need to put in three times the effort of the defendants.

The trial began at 10:30 a.m.

The judge entered the courtroom, and at the clerk's signal, everyone, including the spectators, stood and bowed. After confirming attendance and reviewing the submitted documents under the judge's supervision, the next court date was announced. The session lasted about ten minutes.

It was clear this trial would be a lengthy one. With such a long confinement period and so many defendants, Lawyer Fukumoto estimated "it would likely take at least two years for the first instance judgment." In the end, it took three years from the filing to the first judgment.

The tasks to build the civil case were clear.

I first needed to strengthen my own statement. But I also needed to gather as many witness statements as possible from other victims of abduction and confinement who had been coerced into disaffiliation under the same conditions imposed by Miyamura and Pastor Matsunaga.

I reached out to other victims, met with them to explain the situation, and asked them to write their statements. It must have been painful for them to recall such traumatic experiences, but many victims agreed to help, saying, "If winning this lawsuit can help end abduction and confinement, I will support it." Furthermore, some family members who once acted as perpetrators—e.g., those who had carried out the confinement under Miyamura and Pastor Matsunaga's directions but later regretted their actions—also agreed to write statements. The personal statements from these perpetrators were invaluable and carried tremendous weight as evidence.

I submitted to the court witness statements from ten victims and their family members about Miyamura, and from nine victims and their family members about Pastor Matsunaga.

On the other side, the defendants gave the court the decision notice from the Committee for the Inquest of Prosecution, along with their own statements. Former believers, who had visited the apartments in Niigata and Ogikubo, also provided their witness statements. All of these statements completely denied my abduction and confinement.

This led to a fierce exchange of statements between the plaintiff's side and the defendant's side. I was under constant tension, with no time to rest, as the fourth oral arguments wrapped up in the fall of 2011. Around that time, my wife gave birth to a baby—a joyful moment I could never have imagined during the twelve years and five months of confinement.

While I took comfort in personal happiness with my wife and child, the combative oral arguments continued.

In this trial, I had to put an end to the illegal method of deprograming through abduction and confinement. The root of the problem had to be eradicated.

The perpetrators of abduction and confinement were the believers' families, but they didn't initiate the crimes themselves. Deprograming experts had trained these families in the methods of abduction and confinement, and pushed them to carry out these acts. It was crucial that the wrongdoings of these "deprogrammers"—Miyamura and Pastor Matsunaga—be held accountable.

To do this, I needed to present undeniable evidence showing that Miyamura and Pastor Matsunaga had been systematically teaching and encouraging believers' families to carry out the confinements. Without cutting off the source of this poison, it would be impossible to fully eradicate abduction and confinement.

I had already submitted statements from families who had abducted and confined their children under the guidance of Miyamura and Pastor Matsunaga, but I continued searching for more evidence to expose their wrong actions.

Then, as if fate had prepared it in advance, the evidence surfaced. A manual on confinement and deprograming was discovered.

In 1987, the "National Christian Liaison Council for Counter-measures against the Unification Movement" was founded. The driving force behind it was Pastor Satoshi Moriyama of the Ogikubo Glory Church, a prominent figure in deprograming efforts. Fourteen pastors from around Japan, all dedicated to deprograming activities, attended the inaugural meeting. At that meeting, a manual on forced deprograming was presented, and someone had written it down.

The existence of such a handwritten manual had been rumored for years, but the details had always been unclear. The manual I found was six pages long, each page starting with a heading, followed by a numbered list outlining the methods of abduction, confinement, and forced deprograming.

Excerpts from the manual included:

Page 1 [On Rescuing the Child]

"Create a scene at the house or at a relative's home. Make them realize they have no way to escape. You'll need about six adults for this."

Page 2 [Before Getting in the Car]

"Escape, bathroom breaks, number of people: 5-6 people, 4-5 men. Change locations → move. If the police (110) show up, use 'religious freedom' as a

defense and escape."

Page 4 [On the Parents]

"(1) Do not allow the family to go outside without the persuader's permission. Never let the child (believer) know about (1). Have four people ready for the first week, then reduce it to three. Once the individual declares their disaffiliation over the phone and their belongings are taken, two people should be enough. However, without the persuader's permission, family will not be allowed to leave. There is no doubt the child will escape.

Page 5 [While Persuading]

"Cut off all contact with the outside world. As soon as the believer realizes that someone from the church is nearby, they stop listening and regain their confidence. They won't listen unless they truly believe escape is impossible. That's why it's essential to surround them with 4-6 people. Someone should be awake at all times, 24/7."

Page 6 [Criteria—to allow the believer to go out, the following must be met]:

1. *Write a diary: a. Is the attitude sincere? b. Are proper names mentioned? c. Are the names of "spiritual children" or victims included? d. Is there an understanding of the need to save them?*

2. *Is the believer eager to rescue their spiritual children?*

3. *Do they begin discussing the victims?*

4. *Do they pray in the name of Christ?*

5. *Is their expression brighter, and do they start talking more?*

6. *Do they apologize sincerely to their family, particularly their parents?*

7. *Do they offer to help rescue others in a home (church residence)?*

8. *Do they drink alcohol without hesitation?*

This manual specifies how many people are needed to carry out abduction and confinement, even detailing the number of men to be mobilized. It also includes precautions against police intervention, stating that the "persuader" (the "deprogrammer") must approve before anyone—even the parents of the abducted believer—can leave the confinement site.

The manual also states that, without the persuader's permission, believers cannot be allowed to go outside, and during the persuasion process, all external contact must be cut off. To be allowed to leave, the believer must pass various "tests" outlined in the manual.

The language used is so harsh and coercive that it could easily be misunderstood for something written by a criminal organization. The manual clearly shows a complete disregard for the believer's rights, asserting that any means are acceptable to force disaffiliation.

Incidentally, the "spiritual children" mentioned on the Page 6 of the manual refer to the believers who were converted by the confined believer. The manual promotes the idea that ex-believers must also abduct and confine their "spiritual children" to "rescue" them. This is one of the criteria for "judgment" before a confined person is allowed to leave.

As detailed above, the manual meticulously outlines methods to prevent believers from escaping, effective strategies for forcing disaffiliation, and even a "judgment criteria" or "test" for them to be freed from confinement.

Then, who wrote this manual in the notebook?

After obtaining the manual that outlined the methods of

abduction, confinement, and forced disaffiliation, a videotape was discovered. The tape featured Pastor Matsunaga, one of the defendants, giving a lecture while writing on a board. In some part of the video, he explains the methods of forced disaffiliation through abduction and confinement. This discovery was already significant, but what came next was even more astonishing.

As I watched the lecture repeatedly, I realized that the writing on the board was identical to the one in the handwritten manual. I paused the video and compared the two. There was no doubt—the handwriting was a perfect match. Pastor Matsunaga had written the manual himself.

With both the manual and the lecture video, it became clear that Pastor Matsunaga had been instructing and encouraging the families of Unification Church members to carry out abduction and confinement. The weight of this physical evidence was undeniable, and Pastor Matsunaga had no choice but to admit that the manual and video were authentic. Until that point, he had denied any involvement in the abductions and confinements, but this evidence shattered his claims.

At the same time, an important figure emerged to expose the misdeeds of "deprogramming expert" Miyamura.

A former lawyer affiliated with the National Network of Lawyers Against Spiritual Sales (Zenkoku Benren or NNLASS) revealed that Miyamura's deprogramming activities were essentially a money-making scheme disguised as activities to persuade people to leave the group, with the actual activities being abduction, confinement, and coercion. This statement was written and submitted to the court. The lawyer had no personal stake in the plaintiff's case, and as a former member of Zenkoku Benren, he was a legal expert well-versed in the activities of the defendants. His testimony thoroughly dismantled Miyamura's claims.

This document was submitted ahead of the ninth oral argument, which was scheduled for July 24, 2012.

When the defendants appeared in court for the ninth oral argument, their faces clearly showed a sense of despair. The defendants and their representatives had reviewed the video, the manual, and the document exposing Miyamura's actions. With the presentation of such irrefutable evidence, I could feel the scales of justice tipping significantly in our favor as the plaintiff.

Mother's Death

On May 31, 2012, while I was gathering crucial evidence to expose the true nature of Miyamura and Pastor Matsunaga, I received a call from Lawyer Fukumoto. He informed me that my mother had fallen ill and was hospitalized.

"You should go visit her," he advised.

Along with the call, I also received an email containing a document titled "Notice" from Lawyer Fukumoto. The document had been faxed from the offices of Lawyers Yamaguchi and Ogiue, who represented my brother, sister-in-law, and sister. It provided the name and address of a general hospital in Tokyo.

Two and a half years earlier, during the criminal complaint process, my sister had told me that our mother's dementia was worsening. I assumed her condition had become more severe, which led to her hospitalization. However, when I looked at the attached document, I saw that she had been admitted to the gastroenterology department.

I wanted to learn more about my mother's condition, but I couldn't ask my brother or anyone else involved in the legal dispute. So, I explained the situation to the hospital and asked for information about her health. They kindly agreed to provide it. Four days later, on June 4, I went to the hospital where my mother was staying. According to the attending physician in the gastroenterology department, my mother's condition was even more serious than I imagined.

My mother had been suffering from a rare neurodegenerative disease called corticobasal degeneration, which causes the brain to shrink and gradually leads to dementia. She had been receiving treatment at another hospital for several years. This disease typically leaves patients bedridden within five to ten years. Due to persistent fever and anemia, she had been admitted to this hospital for tests about a month ago. By the time she was admitted, she was already unable to walk and nearly unable to communicate. Further tests revealed that she had colon cancer. The cancer was quite advanced, and due to the severity of her condition, surgery to remove the tumor was deemed too risky. Instead, they decided to perform a colostomy.

"How much longer does she live?" I asked.

The answer was that death would come "probably within a year."

Although they said this, they also cautioned me, saying that, depending on her condition, she might pass away soon, even tomorrow.

The nurse led me into the hospital room, where I saw my mother lying in bed, looking completely changed.

"Mom, it's Toru."

I called out to her, but her gaze remained fixed, staring blankly ahead.

A week later, I returned to the hospital with my wife and child. Even though my mother might not recognize them as her son's wife and her grandchild, I really wanted her to meet them. My child was her first grandchild.

We went to the hospital room and stood by my mother's side.

"Mom, this is your grandchild." My wife gently lifted our child to show her. I called out again, this time raising my voice a little.

"Mom, this is your grandchild."

My mother's gaze shifted, and she looked at my wife and daughter. Although her expression remained unchanged and she didn't speak, it seemed like she recognized who they were.

I asked the front desk to contact me if my mother's condition worsened. The nurse explained that they were only able to contact the family's representative, but it seemed like they understood the situation, so I provided them with my phone number.

On September 20, I received a call from Lawyer Fukumoto on my mobile phone.

"Your mother has passed away."

For some unknown reason, the hospital did not contact me

directly. However, Lawyer Fukumoto forwarded a fax from the family's representative lawyer. It stated that my mother had passed away at 7:35 a.m., and her body had been transferred from the hospital to the funeral home. The document also mentioned that I could visit her until 5:00 p.m. that same day.

I went to the funeral home to say my final goodbyes and see my mother's body.

At the funeral home, the staff guided me to the mortuary. The doors of the refrigerated storage, neatly arranged like lockers, were opened, and a metal gurney was pulled out.

"This way," they said.

Covered with a white cloth, my mother's face was beautifully made up, and despite the many hardships she had endured, she wore a peaceful expression.

From a young age, my mother loved and raised me. But just like with my father, I was never truly able to share our heart until the very end. Was there more I could have done for her? In her life, did I only bring her worry and hardship? A wave of indescribable emotions washed over me.

The next day, I received a notice from the family through Lawyer Fukumoto. My brother, sister-in-law, and sister were planning a memorial service at their church in four days. The message concluded with, *"As the family, we would prefer that Toru refrain from attending."*

I chose to honor their wishes, and as a result, I couldn't attend my mother's funeral—just as I had been excluded from my father's.

The Death Throes of the Cornered

By the end of 2012, nearly a year and ten months had passed since the oral arguments began. In the twelfth session, the court determined that both the plaintiff's and defendant's arguments and evidence had been fully presented, and that witness examinations would begin in 2013.

On March 11, 2013, the first day of witness examination, over 130 people lined up outside the Tokyo District Court for the fifty-two available gallery seats. With the growing number of spectators at each session, a lottery system for tickets had been implemented. The hearing was scheduled from 10:00 a.m. to 5:00 p.m., with a break in between.

At 10:00 a.m., the judge entered the courtroom. "Now, we will begin the direct examination of the plaintiff," he announced, his voice echoing through the courtroom.

I left the plaintiff's seat and took my place at the witness stand in the center of the courtroom, facing the judge. "Please read your sworn statement aloud," the judge instructed.

"Please stand up," the court clerk called for everyone in the gallery to stand.

I then read aloud the sworn statement I had signed and stamped. "I swear to tell the truth according to my conscience, and I will not hide anything nor speak falsely."

Once the court clerk instructed everyone to sit, Lawyer Fukumoto stood up, and the direct examination began.

First, I spoke about my brother, the defendant, being abducted off the streets in Tokyo and his subsequent disaffiliation from the

Unification Church. Then, I described my first abduction and confinement at the Keio Plaza Hotel in 1987, followed by the next eight years of interactions with my family. Next, I provided a detailed account of the entire twelve years and five months of confinement that had taken place since 1995.

In Room 804 of the Flower Mansion, I endured slander and insults from Miyamura, former believers, and my family. I told the judge how this pushed me to the brink, sometimes making me feel like I wanted to die. I explained to the judge the immense suffering, frustration, and bitterness I experienced, being stripped of my freedom and treated as though I were less than human.

I talked about my attempts to escape and how I would scream with all my strength, "I'm being held captive! Please call the police!" in a desperate plea for help. I described the violence from my family, who forcibly held me down to prevent my escape. I also shared how I protested with a hunger strike, and how my family subjected me to food deprivation, bringing me to the brink of starvation. I was reduced to scavenging through trash, pushed to the point of death, and caught between life and death. All of these facts revealed the harsh reality of the abduction, confinement, and deprogramming.

The direct examination was completed without incident, and it was time for the lunch break. I nervously asked Lawyer Fukumoto, "How did it go?"

"I think it went well. The real challenge will be this afternoon's cross-examination."

The cross-examination would take four hours, with six defense lawyers, including Hiroshi Yamaguchi, leading the questioning. As expected, it was clear that this would be the most challenging part of the trial.

The cross-examination began with Morio Ogiue, the lawyer for my brother, sister-in-law, and sister. Next would be Lawyer Takashi Yamaguchi, followed by Hiroshi Yamaguchi, the lawyer for Miyamura. Then it would be Lawyer Sou Kimura; Reiko Higashi, the lawyer for Pastor Matsunaga; and finally Lawyer Shuji Nakamura.

It would be a lie to say I wasn't nervous, but I also felt a sense of anticipation. I saw this as my chance to counter their questions with the truth and show the judge where the truth truly lay. Abduction and confinement were undeniable facts, and all I needed to do was speak honestly about my own experiences.

The cross-examination began with a preposterous claim: "The plaintiff was staying in the apartment to evangelize his family and was attempting to convert them to the Unification Church."

This was the claim the defendant's lawyers had fabricated.

It was undeniable that I had been confined. If they insisted they hadn't confined me, they'd have to argue that I stayed in the apartment voluntarily. But then, they would need a reason for my stay, so they resorted to the excuse of me "evangelizing" my family.

In the Unification Church, evangelizing to relatives is referred to as "Tribal Messiah activity." The defendant's lawyers repeatedly tried to frame my time in the apartment as "Tribal Messiah activity," using various tactics and approaches in their questioning.

I had no intention of agreeing to such an absurd claim. Instead, I consistently stuck to the truth, which was that my only desire during confinement was to "regain my freedom."

Since this was the truth, all I had to do was speak it clearly.

Naturally, their argument fell apart.

When I was asked about the abduction, confinement, and the abuse from food deprivation, I made sure to expose the harsh reality of what I had endured. Soon, the defendant's lawyer tried to interrupt, saying, "Okay, that's enough."

"Don't you let him speak? He's still answering," Lawyer Fukumoto quickly intervened.

The defendant's lawyers looked anxious and flustered as they realized that letting me continue would only benefit my case. I could see it in their expressions and tone.

The questioning covered many different topics, but as I had anticipated, things did not go according to the defendants' plan.

It was two hours of direct examination in the morning and four hours of cross-examination in the afternoon. Because of the intense focus that was required—with no time to let my guard down during the sessions—I was completely exhausted afterward. But despite the physical fatigue, I felt uplifted. I was filled with a sense of accomplishment for fighting through it all.

The direct examination, where I honestly shared my personal experiences and feelings, concluded with Lawyer Fukumoto giving me a "passing grade."

On April 8, 2013, the second round of witness examinations took place.

On this day, two individuals took the stand. Both were former believers who, after being coerced into disaffiliation by Miyamura, had been brought to the Flower Mansion, Room 804, to help deprogram me. Both of their testimonies helped my case.

One witness was a female believer. She testified that she had initially left the Unification Church because of her confinement experience, but she had returned to the church because she felt the teachings were correct.

The other witness was Mr. Fumiaki Tada, the author of several books about "unfair business practices," according to the defense lawyers.

Notably, Mr. Tada admitted in his statement that he had conducted disaffiliation persuasion at the Flower Mansion. This led Lawyer Fukumoto to question Mr. Tada about his relationship with Miyamura.

In two of Mr. Tada's books, there were anecdotes about his experiences working at a company with a domineering, one-man boss. In *Still, Will You Quit the Company?* he described how the boss never set any internal regulations regarding paid holidays and made unreasonable complaints about how to park commuting bikes. This led to a big argument, and ultimately, Mr. Tada quit the company.

In another book, *Cliff-Edge 'Self-Help Training' Attack Record*, Mr. Tada wrote of the boss: *"He was a typical authoritarian figure in a small company. Everything he did was forceful. One morning, when I had stomach issues and needed to stay in the restroom, he forbade all staff from using the work restroom in the morning. When I protested, he absurdly told me to go home and use the restroom before coming in. We often fought over such petty things."*

Listening to the testimony, I was shocked to learn that a boss like this actually existed, but it seemed like something Miyamura might actually do. Based on our side's speculation, we wondered "If this tone were just a bit harsher, it would be exactly like Miyamura when he came to the confinement site," and "Could it be that Tada worked for Miyamura's company after being forced to disaffiliate?"

Lawyer Fukumoto, during cross-examination, asked Mr. Tada if the CEO described in his book was Miyamura. Caught off guard, Mr. Tada casually admitted, "Yes, we had a fight. So what?" When Lawyer Fukumoto followed up, saying, "This really shows Miyamura's character," Mr. Tada justified himself, saying "It's wrong to judge someone by just one aspect. A company is about business. It's not the same as persuasion."

Thus, Mr. Tada's testimony turned out to be very helpful in showing the court Miyamura's character.

In his statement and direct examination, Mr. Tada testified about how he abandoned his faith and denied that abduction and confinement were used during the disaffiliation process. However, his sister contributed a memoir to a book co-authored by Miyamura and others, where she—using her real name—vividly described the methods used to persuade her brother to disaffiliate.

In the book, he was taken to the apartment where he exclaimed, "I trusted you, but you betrayed me," "Enough, you took me here without my consent!" and remarked, "Look at this apartment, it's clearly a room used for [de]conversion." When Miyamura arrived to try and persuade him, Mr. Tada angrily demanded, "Do you think this is okay? I'll sue you!" Miyamura responded before he left, "There's no point in talking about it. Stay here until you understand, no matter if it takes five or ten years." But when Mr. Tada stood up and said, "I'm leaving here!" the family intervened, grabbing him to stop him from escaping.

These events closely mirrored my own experiences in the Flower Mansion as well, making it clear that Mr. Tada, too, had been confined there and subjected to disaffiliation persuasion.

During cross-examination, Lawyer Fukumoto referenced this memoir, and Mr. Tada said, "My parents wouldn't let me leave," which exposed the coercive nature of the disaffiliation process. This admission undermined Mr. Tada's earlier claim that he hadn't been confined, likely strengthening the judge's impression that abduction and confinement had indeed taken place.

On May 14, 2013, the third round of witness examinations took place, and my brother took the stand. He appeared to have aged since the trial began.

While he responded smoothly to his own lawyer during direct examination, everything changed during cross-examination. He repeatedly went silent, struggling to answer Lawyer Fukumoto's questions. He deflected with irrelevant stories and kept saying, "I don't remember" or "I don't recall" when pressed. His evasiveness was so apparent that the judge had to step in, saying, "Please answer the questions clearly."

My brother barely looked at the judge, keeping his head down and speaking in a low, weak voice. His voice was so quiet that Lawyer Takashi Yamaguchi, who represented him, had to adjust the microphone at the witness stand.

Growing up, my brother was always a bit domineering, and I was often the target of his bullying during our childhood arguments. However, before I took my university entrance exams, he wrote me a letter of encouragement, saying, *"This will surely be helpful for your future. Let's study."*

My brother was also the one who introduced me to the Unification Church and was always the most devoted to his faith and church activities. My brother was honest, sincere, and had a strong sense of justice, but none of these qualities showed during his time on the witness stand.

I privately wondered if he was being tormented by his conscience every time he spoke words that were so far removed from the truth. Watching him on the witness stand, my heart tightened.

Once my brother's questioning ended, a heavy, oppressive atmosphere seemed to settle over the defendants' side. It wasn't just my brother who lacked spirit. Though I have no expertise in court proceedings, it was clear that not only his answers but also his expressions and demeanor failed to make a positive impression on the judge.

On June 3, 2013, the fourth round of witness examinations took place. On this day, Pastor Matsunaga and my sister-in-law took the stand.

Pastor Matsunaga was questioned by his lawyer about a videotape of one of his lectures. He explained that he had created the video, but after receiving negative feedback from former believers and their families, he decided to stop using it. Next, he was asked about the handwritten manual on abduction and confinement. He insisted that he had merely transcribed the speaker's words and that the ideas were not his own.

During cross-examination, Lawyer Fukumoto presented multiple pieces of evidence showing Pastor Matsunaga's direct involvement in inciting and instructing abduction and confinement. Pastor Matsunaga tried to deflect responsibility, claiming, "It's up to the family to decide" and "It's not my responsibility."

This wasn't just an attempt to shift the blame onto my family, but he was also putting blame on all the families of the believers and refusing to take any responsibility himself. His reckless and irresponsible attitude infuriated me.

In the afternoon, my sister-in-law took the stand.

During cross-examination, she struggled to answer several questions, but after observing my brother's cross-examination, perhaps she learned how to give only evasive answers. She repeatedly answered questions with "I don't know" or "I'm not sure."

On June 17, 2013, the witness examinations concluded. The last witnesses were my sister and Miyamura.

In the morning, my sister took the stand. Since she was the

one who usually prepared the meals, Lawyer Fukumoto asked her about the connection between food deprivation and abuse. My sister insisted that she had always been mindful of my health and had prepared separate meals for me, apart from the rest of the family. But when inconvenient questions were asked, she, like my sister-in-law, simply said, "I don't remember."

In the afternoon, Miyamura took the stand.

During direct examination by his lawyer, Miyamura confidently explained his philosophy and counseling methods as a "rescue" counselor. He insisted that he did not use force and always respected the will of the believers, claiming that he had never provided guidance on abduction or confinement.

However, when Lawyer Fukumoto began the cross-examination, Miyamura's demeanor shifted to one of arrogance. He mocked the questions, saying, "Please make sure to collect proper evidence, then ask me," and "Mr. Fukumoto, please stop such poor leading questions." He also made irregular remarks like, "Do you understand Japanese, sir?" This behavior also appeared to be seen by the judge as arrogant and insincere. The judge sternly warned, "We'll take note of this exactly in the record."

Miyamura's attitude and demeanor in court mirrored the behavior I had witnessed daily at the Flower Mansion. The many years he spent forcing Unification Church members to disaffiliate had clearly shaped his character, and this was evident in his actions during the trial. It appeared that the defendant's testimony, including Miyamura's arrogant responses, only worsened the judge's perception of the defense.

On September 24, 2013, the final oral arguments took place. On that day, the last claims were made, and after two years and eight months of proceedings since the civil lawsuit was filed, the first phase of the trial concluded. All that remained was to wait for the verdict.

The Incomplete Victory in Court

On January 28, 2014, the day of the first trial's judgment arrived.

The weather in Tokyo was clear, with unusually warm temperatures for midwinter, reaching 15°C during the day. At 3:00 p.m., the judgment was to be announced in Courtroom 709. When I arrived at the Tokyo District Court about thirty minutes before the trial, there was already a crowd gathered, hoping to get tickets for the public gallery. Equal numbers of supporters of the plaintiff and the defendants seemed to be there.

"Goto-san, finally it's the day of judgment," I heard from supporters, who were unable to hide their excitement.

The tension within me increased. When I entered Courtroom 709, Lawyer Fukumoto was already there. The defendants and their representatives were seated in the defendant's area, waiting for the judgment with tense expressions.

At the scheduled time, Judge Tetsu Aizawa entered the courtroom and promptly read the summary of the judgment aloud.

"The defendant (brother), the defendant (sister-in-law), and the defendant (sister) are ordered to jointly pay the plaintiff 4,839,910 yen, along with 5% annual interest starting from February 10,

2008, until full payment is made..."

Once Judge Aizawa finished reading the judgment, the court session was adjourned.

The judgment stated that my brother, sister-in-law, and sister were required to pay a total of 4.83 million yen, with Miyamura responsible for 960,000 yen of that amount.

Since the summary reading by the judge was somewhat unclear, I asked Lawyer Fukumoto for his assessment after we left the courtroom.

"I can't say much until I see the full judgment, but at least we've won, in part," he told me.

Although it was only a partial victory, a win is still a win. For the moment, I felt a wave of relief.

After the judgment was announced, we were scheduled to immediately report the result to our supporters in front of the Tokyo District Court. Over 100 supporters had gathered in front of the court's main entrance. When I shared the news of our victory, a loud cheer erupted from the crowd. The scene was broadcast live on the internet, reaching supporters both in Japan and around the world.

At 5:00 p.m., a press conference was held at the Judicial Press Club, and the following day, January 29, major media outlets covered the event. The Asahi Shimbun reported on the social page, stating, *"Unification Church follower wins case against family,"* and noted, *"Judge Tetsu Aizawa ruled that 'the family had severely restricted the man's freedom for an extended period' and ordered them to pay approximately 4.8 million yen."* The Sankei Shimbun's Osaka edition reported,

"Persuading Disaffiliation from the Unification Church: Family Ordered to Pay 4.8 Million Yen in Damages" and quoted *"Judge Tetsu Aizawa stated in the reasoning for the judgment that 'the act of significantly restricting an adult's freedom to persuade them goes beyond the limits of social norms.'"*

After reading the sixty-five-page judgment, I realized that while we had won partially, the decision was far from a complete victory.

The court acknowledged that Miyamura and Pastor Matsunaga had instructed the families of the believers to restrict their freedom in an attempt to persuade them to disaffiliate, and that I was not allowed to leave freely from the apartments in Niigata and Tokyo. It was also recognized that the defendants' actions were coercive.

However, the court accepted the defendant's claim that I reluctantly agreed to go with them to the Niigata apartment. This led to the conclusion that the defendants' actions at the first apartments in Niigata and Tokyo were not considered illegal. As a result, Pastor Matsunaga was not held responsible for the disaffiliation persuasion at the first apartment. Only the actions of Miyamura at the third apartment, where he partially involved my family in preventing my departure, were deemed illegal.

I appreciated the judgment for recognizing that Miyamura and Pastor Matsunaga had systematically instructed the families of believers to restrict their freedom in order to persuade them to disaffiliate. I also valued the acknowledgment of the responsibility of my brother, sister-in-law, younger sister, and Miyamura for their actions at the Flower Mansion.

However, I disagreed with the denial of Pastor Matsunaga's full responsibility and the partial acknowledgment of Miyamura's, and the failure to recognize the abuse caused by food deprivation. I also found that the duration of the confinement and deprogramming was recognized as approximately ten years instead of the actual twelve years and five months. And the emotional distress compensation was only 4.83 million yen. I was deeply dissatisfied with these results, which showed a significant lack of consideration for human rights.

After consulting with Lawyer Fukumoto, I decided to appeal the case to the Tokyo High Court. The defendants, who had lost the case, also filed an appeal. With both sides appealing, the case moved to the second instance.

The Battle of Twelve Years and Five Months— Plus Seven Years

On June 5, 2014, the first oral arguments in the appeals court took place. In preparation for this session, I had focused on preparing evidence, including written statements, to address the issues that were not acknowledged in the first trial.

However, during the oral arguments, the defendants presented unexpected evidence. I was taken aback when I saw the document that Lawyer Fukumoto had sent me.

The scrap of paper was densely packed with tiny writing.

About a year before I was released from the Flower Mansion, when I was mentally and physically pushed to the brink, I had written down the message I received from God on that piece of calendar paper. In the dark early hours of the morning, in a Japanese-style room, I desperately prayed. Worrying about the dwindling lead in my mechanical pencil as I wrote down my thoughts, these words, filled with desperation, were now being submitted as evidence by the defendants.

This piece of paper is numbered "Defendant's Exhibit II-49" in the evidence explanation document and is called a "calendar scrap." In the defendant's "Proof Objective," the following was written:

"The plaintiff in the first trial wrote on the calendar paper scrap that, 'Still, love them! This is My heart. As their Messiah, love them, love them, love them, and save them! Save them! Don't hesitate! Love and save them!' This suggests that while at the Flower Mansion, the plaintiff, as a Unification Church believer, was driven by his faith as a 'Tribal Messiah' and had the desire to save the defendant of first instance (brother) and his family, which was why he stayed in the mansion."

This claim was so absurd that I had to smile wryly.

The defendants had repeatedly insisted, in a ridiculous manner, that I was "staying in the apartment to evangelize to my family and convert them to the Unification Church." Since this argument had been completely dismissed in the first trial, they presented the "calendar scrap" as evidence at this late stage.

I gazed at the paper scrap once more, carefully examining the tiny, densely packed words.

The memories from that time came rushing back.

By that time, ten years had passed since my confinement, and I was forty-three years old. In a state of extreme conditions, enduring loneliness, despair, and hunger, my hatred was on the verge of spiraling out of control. It was during those days that I clung to God in prayer. Amidst my desperate prayers, I felt God's presence and realized I had not been abandoned. God gave me hope and courage. The calendar scrap was where I had written down the revelation I received from God.

The small, tightly packed handwriting on the paper reminded me of letters written in prison. In fact, the calendar scrap turned out to be a powerful piece of evidence that backed my claims. Nothing is more convincing than the truth. I could only think of it as a miracle that the calendar scrap had resurfaced now. More than anything, I was truly happy to be reunited with a piece of paper I had thought was lost forever. By cutting out only a portion of the full text, the defendants tried to use it to suit their own narrative, and in doing so, they dug their own grave.

I transcribed the entire message from the calendar scrap and started drafting a statement to explain and provide context. Through the words written on that paper, I was able to show just how harsh the conditions I endured at the time were.

For example, the phrase on the scrap that says, *"opposition, persecution, bullying, and many struggles—be happy the more intense they become,"* reflects the growing intensity of the "opposition, persecution, bullying, and struggles" I faced during more than ten years of confinement, where I was deprived of proper meals. God's revelation was a kind of scolding that urged me to embrace these hardships with strength and acceptance. The reason I was able to endure these extreme conditions without completely losing my mental stability was because of the hope and courage I drew from these divine messages.

The statement made by my brother and others, claiming that I stayed in the mansion to save my family, with words like *"Still, love them! …love them, love them, and save them! Love and save them!"* was not my sentiment, but rather a "God's message." In the midst of my hatred, which was on the verge of spiraling out of control, this divine message allowed me to understand God's profound love—something far beyond human comprehension. Because of that, I was able to maintain my mental stability during such extreme conditions.

At that time, I was denied even basic supplies, such as notebooks and mechanical pencil leads. This forced me to use a scrap of calendar paper, writing in tiny letters to conserve lead. If I had been free at that time, I could have easily gone out and bought the necessary supplies. Therefore, the fact that I had to write in such small handwriting on this calendar paper is a crucial piece of evidence proving that I was being confined.

I included these claims in a twenty-page statement, which I submitted.

In July 2014, more positive news arrived.

The Human Rights Committee of the United Nations European Headquarters expressed concerns about the "abductions and forced confinement of converts to new religious movements in an effort to de-convert them" in Japan and called on the Japanese government to take effective measures to guarantee the right of every person.

Below is an excerpt from the Human Rights Committee's "Concluding Observations on the Sixth Periodic Report of Japan" from August 20, 2014:

[Abduction and forced de-conversion] 21. The Committee is concerned at reports of abductions and forced confinement of converts to new religious movements by members of their families in an effort to de-convert them (arts. 2, 9, 18, 26). The State party should take effective measures to guarantee the right of every person not to be subject to coercion that would impair his or her freedom to have or to adopt a religion or belief.

The Human Rights Committee had reviewed and reported on Japan's human rights situation six times as of 2014. However, this was the first time that the issue of "abduction and forced confinement of converts to new religious movements by members of their families in an effort to de-convert them" was addressed. With the United Nations' recommendation to the Japanese government, the court had no choice but to take it seriously.

Furthermore, the Human Rights Committee reviews the human rights conditions of 193 member states, and Japan's review only comes around once every six or seven years. The year 2014 was when the report on Japan was made public, and just before the appellate trial concluded. Of course, the report was submitted to the court.

On the other hand, the defendants failed to present any significant new evidence and simply repeated their claims from the first trial.

On August 21, 2014, the second oral arguments took place. The appellate trial was then concluded and the waiting period for the ruling began.

On November 13, 2014, the day of the judgment arrived.

I entered the courtroom and took my seat as the plaintiff. Soon after, Lawyer Fukumoto entered and sat beside me. Looking at the defendant's seat, I saw them chatting, and Pastor Matsunaga, who had been absent during the previous oral arguments, had traveled from Niigata to attend. The public gallery, with forty-two seats, was filled to capacity by those who had managed to obtain tickets through a highly competitive three-to-one lottery.

At 2:30 p.m., the three judges entered the courtroom.

"Now, we will announce the judgment," Presiding Judge Noriaki Sudo declared solemnly and then proceeded to read the main text of the judgment.

"Main text: 1. Based on the appellant's appeal, the original judgment is amended as follows."

The three defendants—my brother, sister-in-law, and younger sister—were ordered to pay a total of 22 million yen, while Miyamura was ordered to pay 11 million yen of the damages above, and Pastor Matsunaga was ordered to pay 4.4 million yen of them.

It could be said that my claims were largely accepted.

Presiding Judge Sudo read the main text of the judgment

calmly. While in civil court, judgments typically end with just the case number and the main text, but Judge Sudo took the time to explain the essence of the ruling, which was difficult to understand due to the legal jargon.

Based on the notes I took in the courtroom, here is a summary of what Judge Sudo explained:

When family members try to persuade a family who has joined a religious group, it is not automatically illegal if the individual agrees. However, even within a family, a person's freedom of will and dignity must be respected. If the person refuses to be persuaded, attempting to convince them by restricting their freedom of movement is generally considered illegal, unless the person voluntarily consents.

In this case, the appellant (the plaintiff) was thirty-one years old and an adult at the time. Despite the relationship between family, the individual's will and freedom must be fully respected. Although it is the father's strong desire for the appellant to disaffiliate from the Unification Church, and this led the brother and others to act out of familial love, unless the individual voluntarily agrees, any actions that exceed reasonable limits will be deemed illegal.

Furthermore, in this case, the appellant had previously been "persuaded" but had escaped and did not disaffiliate. As a result, the family anticipated that the appellant would not easily agree to persuasion, so they took additional steps, such as seeking support, preparing a van and portable toilet to prevent the appellant from escaping, and taking him to Niigata. Therefore, it can be recognized that, from the outset, the persuasion was intended to restrict the appellant's free will and actions.

At both the Niigata apartment and the two apartments in Ogikubo, the family took the appellant's belongings, restricted his freedom to leave, and prevented him from making phone calls. Even when the appellant prepared a letter of disaffiliation, the family continued to limit his freedom of movement, suspecting it was a false disaffiliation. This ongoing illegal situation can be clearly recognized.

Although the appellant was repeatedly pressured to disaffiliate, the appellant did not show the desired response. Finally, the family decided to expel the appellant on February 10, 2008, abandoning the persuasion efforts. Thus, the court confirmed that until that point, the illegal restriction of the appellant's freedom had continued.

In practice, it was the appellant's family who lived with him, restricted his freedom, and effectively confined him. However, the family had turned to Miyamura and Pastor Matsunaga from the outset, seeking their teachings and guidance on how to carry out the disaffiliation process. While Miyamura and Pastor Matsunaga did not directly restrict the appellant's freedom, it can be concluded that they encouraged and assisted the series of illegal actions against the appellant and were fully aware of what the family was doing.

Additionally, Pastor Matsunaga and Miyamura had encouraged

the appellant to disaffiliate, endorsing the actions of the appellant's family and providing them with the mental backing for their behavior over the years. As a result, it is only fair to hold them accountable for the illegal acts committed against the appellant, alongside the family.

The restriction of freedom lasted a full twelve years and five months. During this time, the appellant lost crucial years of his life, from the age of thirty-one to forty-four, a period that should have been filled with opportunities. The defendants were significantly responsible for this.

The result was a victory that surpassed the first trial.

When the session ended, Lawyer Fukumoto smiled and said, "I'm glad for you." I exchanged firm handshakes with the supporters who had gathered. Meanwhile, the defendants were sitting in stunned silence, clearly in disbelief. They even canceled the press conference scheduled for 3:00 p.m. at the Judicial Press Club.

It was clear that they had fully realized their defeat.

In the first trial, the illegality of the confinement in the first and second apartments was not acknowledged. However, in the court of second instance, it was recognized that the confinement in all three apartments, spanning the entire twelve years and five months, was illegal.

Moreover, Pastor Matsunaga's responsibility and the illegality of his actions, which had not been addressed in the first trial, were now recognized, along with the abuse resulting from food deprivation. Additionally, the damages for emotional distress were significantly increased to 22 million yen.

This ruling can be considered a **complete victory**, as almost all of our claims were upheld.

I recalled how in the criminal case I filed, the Committees for the Inquest of Prosecution's decision had largely sided with the defendants. But, thankfully, in the civil lawsuit, the outcome was completely different.

Afterward, my brother, sister-in-law, younger sister, Miyamura, and Pastor Matsunaga, who had lost in the second instance, all appealed to the Supreme Court.

It is extremely rare for a judgment to be overturned by the Supreme Court. The Supreme Court generally does not reexamine the facts of a case but instead addresses legal issues, such as violations of the Constitution, prior Supreme Court rulings, or misinterpretations of the law. There were no legal or procedural errors in the earlier trials, but I still had to stay on alert.

On September 29, 2015, ten months after the judgment of the second instance, the Supreme Court rejected the defendants' appeal. The second instance's judgment was thus finalized, bringing the case to a close.

It had been four years and nine months since the civil lawsuit was filed. Including the criminal complaint, the legal battle over the abduction and confinement case had lasted more than seven years.

The year following the finalization of winning of the judgment—2016—became a pivotal year for the Unification Church in Japan. For the first time since the abduction and confinement incidents began in 1966, it became a year when there were **zero abductions and confinements**.

I spent twenty years of my life battling against abduction and confinement, a fight not only for my own freedom but also to put an end to such illegal practices.

Whether in the battle under confinement or the battle in court, I faced immense challenges that left me crushed by despair and setbacks. I can't even count how many times I was saved by miraculous events. Each time, I felt the love and guidance of a living God that went far beyond human strength. I truly believe that the fight to eradicate abduction and confinement was a battle "guided by God."

Chapter 5

The Abductions and Confinements Have Not Ended

Since the 2015 Supreme Court ruling in my case, incidents of believers being abducted and confined have become rare. However, they have not entirely stopped.

In January 2021, a young believer in his twenties was confined in his home in Kanagawa Prefecture for about a month. He managed to escape by removing the louvered window of the bathroom on the second floor. Moreover, in January 2024, a young believer in his twenties in Tokyo was subjected to forced disaffiliation and, while under confinement, coerced into abandoning his faith. Moreover, no one should forget the presence of victims who developed PTSD because of abduction and confinement and who continue to suffer from its effects to this day.

Today, the Japanese government is trying to dissolve and liquidate the Unification Church. The case is now in the hands of the courts. However, many believers are concerned that if the church is dissolved, the harmful effects of abduction and confinement might resurface and spread across the country, just as they did in the past.

These developments are not only known to those directly involved but are also becoming more public.

Since the assassination of former Prime Minister Shinzo Abe in 2022, media outlets have ramped up their critical coverage of the Unification Church. Numerous so-called "victims" and "experts" have come forward, and the church has now been widely labeled as an "antisocial organization."

My sister-in-law, who lost the lawsuit in my case and whose illegal actions were recognized, appeared on TBS's *Hodo Tokusyu (Report Special)* (aired in August 2022) as a former believer. She once again harshly criticized the Unification Church, repeating lies in the same manner she had when she tried to force me to disaffiliate in the confinement room.

Similarly, Takashi Miyamura, who also lost the lawsuit and whose illegal actions were acknowledged, was invited in August 2022 to a meeting of the Constitutional Democratic Party of Japan under the guise of "hearing from a disaffiliation supporter." There, he lectured members of Parliament on his anti-Unification Church stance. During the meeting, Yoshifu Arita, a close ally of Miyamura, praised his efforts, saying, "He has made significant contributions to helping many believers disaffiliate."

The perpetrators who were ordered to pay 22 million yen in damages for abducting and confining me for twelve years and five months, as well as those found guilty of aiding and abetting them, appeared on television and lectured members of Parliament as if nothing had happened. This was nothing short of outrageous.

Moreover, it is widely known that among the past civil cases used by the government to justify their request for a dissolution order, many of the cases were filed by former believers who were forcibly disaffiliated through abduction. Meanwhile, there was no media coverage of the abductions and confinements that many Unification Church members had suffered, including my own case.

The issue of abduction and confinement has not ended.

What is the truth? Should the Unification Church truly be dissolved? I hope that readers will be able to confirm the "truth" for themselves, using their own eyes and ears.

Now, I would like to provide further explanation on the deprogrammers who carried out the disaffiliation persuasion, a topic that wasn't fully addressed in the main text, and shed light on the details of abduction, confinement, and disaffiliation.

This book reflects on the extreme human rights violations and legal battles, and how not only my life but the lives of countless others were destroyed by these deprogrammers. Some readers may find it difficult to believe these things, However, more details about in-depth experiences and analyses of abduction, confinement, and disaffiliation are in Hirohisa Koide's book, *Escape from the Kidnapper* (Kogen-sha) and Yutaka Toriumi's *250 Days of Confinement: Complete Testimony of Deprogramming* (Kogen-sha).

Let's begin with Pastor Yasutomo Matsunaga of the Niitsu Evangelical Church, who came to persuade me in Niigata.

According to the *Escape from the Kidnapper*, his church is described as being located in a three-story building with a total area of 600 tsubo (around 2,000 square meters). To construct this church, they borrowed 100 million yen from Sanwa Bank (at the time), and the rest was supposed to be funded by donations from the Evangelical Church believers. However, the donations were only around 400,000 yen per month, barely enough to cover the bank's repayment obligations.

As a result, Pastor Matsunaga frequently requested donations and loans from former Unification Church believers and their families through written letters. Mr. Koide's father, who had long relied on Miyamura for guidance, was also told by Miyamura, "It's an offering, offering. You could just give it as an offering, right?" leading him to provide 1 million yen as a donation and 3 million yen as a loan.

Mr. Koide wrote, *"From the realistic demands of fundraising for the new church building, I believe Pastor Matsunaga had no choice but to become deeply involved in the 'anti-Unification Church movement' rather than focusing solely on the 'salvation from sin through Christ's redemption.'"*

Next, regarding Takashi Miyamura, it can be said that he played a key role in intensifying the disaffiliation activities being carried out at Pastor Satoshi Moriyama's Ogikubo Glory Church.

Miyamura was not a Christian, but his wife was a member of the Ogikubo Glory Church. The daughter of Miyamura's mentor became a Unification Church believer, and it was through this consultation that he came into contact with Pastor Moriyama, as explained in *250 Days of Confinement: Complete Testimony of Deprogramming.*

Miyamura would have parents who wanted their children to disaffiliate join a membership-based group he ran, called *Mizuku-ki-kai* (water stem society). Within the group, an interview was conducted to thoroughly evaluate the following criteria: 1) whether the parents were desperate, 2) whether they were willing to follow Miyamura and the group's instructions on abduction and confinement, 3) whether they regularly attended the group's meetings, 4) whether other siblings had also started attending the meetings, 5) Whether the parents were determined to get their child back, even if it meant losing their home and property, including their jobs, 6) whether relatives were cooperative, and 7) whether the child could meet with their parents upon returning home.

Once the preparations were made, an apartment in which Mizukuki-kai had made contracts would be assigned for the confinement. In very difficult cases, a hotel room was used.

The rent for the confinement rooms was paid by the family using the room for confinement. When the family moved out, the next family to use the room would pay the rent. The furniture in the room was often left behind by previous family, and it seemed as though the rooms were shared in a cooperative manner. If the confinement attempt failed, due to an escape, the room would be left unused for a period, and the rent would be covered by the membership fees of the Mizukuki-kai.

As Yutaka Toriumi pointed out in his book, not only was the sub-lease suspicious, but the complete lack of transparency regarding the contracts raises serious concerns.

Miyamura's advertising agency transformed into a unique entity in the early 1990s, with all of its employees being former Unification Church members. One of those employees was my brother. Miyamura, who was known for his left-wing student activism, was undoubtedly a complicated and difficult person to deal with.

Both Pastor Matsunaga and Miyamura, along with many others who took on the task of "rescuing" Unification Church members across Japan, were mostly Christian pastors. It seems that many of them still view the forced disaffiliation they carried out as "a good thing." In Western countries, not only is deprogramming illegal, but abduction and confinement are also recognized as crimes that are widely condemned and unforgivable in society. Forced disaffiliation through abduction and confinement is a criminal act—and until this obvious truth is fully understood in Japanese society, the battle is far from over.

I would like to conclude this book by introducing the late Asako Shukuya, also a victim of abduction and confinement.

Throughout my trial, the support from my fellow believers and former believers who had also been abducted and forcibly disaffiliated was a tremendous source of strength. Among them, Asako Shukuya, who endured PTSD for many years as a result of abduction and confinement, played a crucial role.

Asako is featured prominently in Kazuhiro Yonemoto's book, *Our Unpleasant Neighbor,* in which he captured a photograph of my bare and emaciated body. Despite her criticism of the Unification Church, Asako volunteered to assist with my trial, saying she would do it "if it's for the eradication of abduction and confinement." She went on to create a website, called *Yozakura-an(夜桜 餡)*, where she shared her own struggles with PTSD and worked tirelessly to raise awareness of the profound and lasting damage that abduction and confinement can cause to both the mind and body. She listened to the voices of victims suffering from the after-effects of abduction and confinement, and she dedicated herself to helping them recover both physically and mentally. For Asako, it didn't matter whether the victims were believers or not; she was focused solely on their suffering and their healing. Her PTSD began to recover and she made a successful return to society.

However, on October 15, 2012, she passed away at the age of forty-eight due to a subarachnoid hemorrhage. Despite having disaffiliated from the Unification Church, she continued to stand by the victims of abduction and confinement, offering them compassion and support. I am truly grateful for everything she did.

A Chronology of the 12 Years and 5 Months of Abduction and Confinement

September 11, 1995 Night (Age 31)	Abducted from my family's home in Tokyo and confined on the sixth floor of an apartment in Niigata. Pastor Yasutomo Matsunaga of the Niitsu Evangelical Church and former believers visited the apartment and conducted deprogramming sessions.
June 1997	Following my father's death, I was moved from the apartment in Niigata to another confinement site on the sixth floor of a Tokyo apartment (2nd location).
December 1997	Transferred to a different confinement site on the eighth floor of another apartment in Tokyo (3rd location).
January 1998	Mr. Takashi Miyamura, a deprogrammer, visited with former believers to conduct deprogramming sessions. Despite suffering from influenza and a fever approaching 40°C, I was not allowed to see a doctor.
February 2001	Terrified by the sense of being cut off from the outside world, I repeatedly shouted for help. Though I tried several times to escape, I was physically restrained by my family and Mr. Miyamura. Unable to visit a dentist, I became obsessed with brushing my teeth out of fear of developing cavities.
November 2003	I faintly heard the voice of a speaker calling out, "To the residents of Ogikubo 3-chome, this is Nobuteru Ishihara speaking" from outside. This was the moment when I finally learned my location.

April 2004	In protest against my confinement, I carried out a three-week hunger strike.
April 2005	I undertook a second three-week hunger strike.
April 2006	I launched a third hunger strike, this time for one month. I was subjected to abuse for one year and ten months, during which I was given only minimal amounts of food.
December 2006	In a state of severe mental and physical exhaustion, I began praying early every morning. I wrote down messages from God on a scrap of calendar paper.
February 10, 2008 Evening (Age 44)	I was suddenly expelled from the confinement apartment with nothing but the clothes on my back and no money at all. With nowhere to go, I set out on foot toward the church headquarters ten kilometers away. However, I soon became unable to walk. That night, I cried out for help on the roadside, and by a miraculous coincidence, the woman who responded was a member of the Unification Church. Thanks to her, I was brought to the church headquarters and was urgently hospitalized for emergency treatment.

Acknowledgments

Many people encouraged me with the preparation of this book. I would like to thank Universal Peace Federation-Japan Secretary General Shunsuke Uotani for his special assistance and President Tomihiro Tanaka of the Family Federation for World Peace and Unification-Japan, who provided invaluable support for this book. I sincerely appreciate Ms. Tamami Nozoe for her masterful work translating the Japanese version to English, and Cheryl Wetzstein for her assistance in perfecting the English. I am grateful for Jonathan Gullery's skillful design and layout and the efforts of Thomas McDevitt and Henri Schauffler of the Times Global Media Group for assisting with its publication.

I also wish to honor the support of Mamoru Kamono, Fumihiro Kato and many others for their sincere efforts to help bring my story to the world.

Toru Goto
Tokyo, Japan
July 2025